E TIMES FRIDAY SEPTEMBER 29

W9-BBE-409

MPA

Domenica 24 Settembre 1967

LA PIU' DECISA NEMICA DEI COLONNELLI

con la coraggiosa signora greca
ue mesi sfida i militari al potere

(ancora in libertà) di tutta la Grecia che abbia detto apertamente no al nuovo regime - Proprietaria di due influenti giornali,

subjected by the Government beside
financial ones ?

"The strongest ones have com
from one of my former contributor
Mr. Papakostantinou. He was
good columnist, a specialist
writing articles against dictator
Then the colonels arrived on th
scene. One morning, after I ha
stopped the newspapers, he came
me and said, ' Madam, somethi
terrible is happening. They want
appoint me deputy of Papadopoul
in his Ministry. Where can I hide
' Take time ', I replied, ' try and di
cuss this proposal '. ' But when I se
them I feel like vomiting '."

Not defending
the past

" Maybe Mr. Papakostantinou w
not like this memory, but unfo
tunately for him the conversatic
was recorded. Two months afte
wards he telephoned me. ' Madar
I have decided to accept. And
have promised the Government th
you will publish. Please trust m
I give you my word that, as soc
as the newspapers will be on sal
the freedom of the press will b
reinstated.' "

"' My dear friend ', I told hir
' maybe I can trust you but not th
colonels. First proclaim the fre
dom of the press, then we shall see
Since then two months have gor
by and I am still waiting for th
announcement."

How do you think this story w
end ?

" I have no idea, ask the colone
Perhaps they lose patience and or
evening they will have me arreste
by the police. May be, I do n
know, they will become ashamed
the poor show they are making
the world and the press will becon
free again, at least in part. If th
happens, the Greeks too will
able to read certain truths. I a

HOUSE ARREST

Helen Vlachos at her desk in the *Kathimerini* office on Socrates Street.

HOUSE ARREST

HELEN VLACHOS

Gambit
INCORPORATED
Boston
1970

FIRST PRINTING

© Copyright 1970 by Helen Vlachos
All rights reserved, including the right to reproduce this book or parts
thereof in any form
Library of Congress Catalog Card Number: 78-113839
Printed in the United States of America

Published in Great Britain, 1970, by André Deutsch Limited, London

Author's Note

After my arrival in London, I was asked hundreds of questions about Greece and the Junta, and just one about myself. What was my name? Helen Vlachos, Helen Vlachou, or Eleni Vlachou? To that question there was no answer, as Greek grammar and Greek tradition differ peacefully on the subject.

Greek grammar declines proper names and rules that any female relative of a man whose name ends with "*os*," being "his," must take the possessive ending "*ou*." That is, you have Mr. Vlach*os* and Mrs. or Miss Vlach*ou*, Mr. Venisel*os* and Mrs. Venisel*ou*, and so on. But out of Greece, the rules of grammar are automatically dropped, and (probably for the benefit of the bank manager or the hotel porter) the masculine nominative is used by all the members of the family, male or female.

So I was Eleni Vlachou in Greece, and Helen Vlachos out of Greece, and while I kept the name professionally through two marriages, I never had any trouble with it until now. All traveling Greeks do the same, changing from the Greek form to the foreign form without giving the matter a second thought. Both are considered right at different times and places.

That is one of the reasons I continue to use, out of Greece, "Helen Vlachos." The other reason is that I have found long ago that I could make my name better remembered by counseling: "Just think of the words 'black horse' and pronounce them very softly." I still have friends met ten or twenty years ago who remember me as someone approximately called "Blackoss" or "Vlachorse."

CONTENTS

ILLUSTRATIONS

Photo by Helen Vlachos

"We don't need a warrant"

ATHENS: *October 4, 1967*

A sudden uproar woke us up.

It was seven o'clock in the morning. People were banging at the door of our flat and at the same time ringing the bell continuously. The two dachshunds joined in the din by barking hysterically, and our first thought was that the house was on fire.

We jumped out of bed, ran to the little entrance hall, and opened the door. Three unknown men stood outside.

They immediately filed in, in solid, unsmiling silence. The first to enter, thin, dark, fortyish, was wearing a blue suit, a wisp of a moustache on a hatchet face, and an air of importance. The other two, dressed in grubby shirts and trousers, stayed a pace or two behind. One was a young, fair, pimply youth, the other a mountain of a man with a large, red, brutish face.

"Security Police," the blue suit announced. "We have orders to search the premises."

"Have you got a warrant?"

"We don't need a warrant."

"Have you got any identification papers?" my husband insisted. "How do we know you are Security Police?"

The man smiled pityingly.

I

"*You* don't need to know anything. *We* are the ones who have to know."

I have not changed one word of this laconic dialogue that marked the beginning of the period of our house arrest, and I don't think I shall ever forget this terrifyingly simple exposition of what a totalitarian regime means in everyday life.

You, until a short time ago a responsible individual, have lost all your rights; *you* "don't need to know anything any more"; *you* are not entitled to any excuses or explanations; *you* are on the receiving end of orders coming from *them*.

The flat where my husband and I had lived since our marriage in 1951 was a small sixth-floor penthouse at the corner of Mourouzi and Herod Atticus streets. It had two bedrooms, a large living room, and a small dining room with French windows opening onto a wide terrace. During the day we spent very few hours there, as the *Kathimerini* building on Socrates Street combined the facilities of both a house and an office. The Vlachos family house, built around the middle of the nineteenth century, had been pulled down in 1953 and had given place to modern and spacious newspaper offices. But we had kept the whole top floor as a reception area, with large drawing rooms that had collected all the best furniture, paintings, and books of three generations of the Vlachos family, and we also had a small but adequate projection room, where we had frequent private shows of the latest movies. So that even after we had suspended the publication of the newspapers, we kept on going there, morning and afternoon, meeting friends, colleagues, Greek and foreign journalists and visitors. All our papers, our books, all documents that could be of any interest were kept at Socrates Street, and any "search" should have chosen the *Kathimerini* building as a starting point.

But it soon appeared that it was not a real search but just an exercise in naïve, deliberate, and nonetheless infuriating provocation.

"You look around the books—" blue-suit ordered the younger man, and then, turning to number three: "You keep guard at the door, and see that no one gets in."

He then proceeded to mess about.

It was quite plain that he did not know what to look for, that he did not understand what he was reading, and that he had no reason to put this letter or memo or bill aside instead of that one. But while his companion was opening and shaking whatever books he found, he went on doggedly pulling out drawers and emptying them on the carpet. He looked with grim suspicion at a collection of tapes he discovered near a cabinet full of gramophone records, chose some at random, and put them aside.

He shuffled through every nook and cranny, meanwhile keeping up a steady stream of monologue. He was the only one who spoke, in a disagreeable, toneless, whining voice, using the third person in an effort to sound impersonal.

". . . From today the Kyria Eleni Vlachou is under house arrest." He did not know why, or for how long. His orders were to put guards outside the front doors and forbid any kind of communication with anyone. Also the telephone had been disconnected since morning. And no post would be delivered. Now he was to collect what "suspect" documents or photos or letters he could find and take them down to Police Headquarters. They would be inspected there, and returned. We were to count them, so that we could not say later that anything had been stolen. The Kyrios Costas Loundras was free to come and go, and so was the service. But they must be very careful not to try and pass any messages from the Kyria, because they could get into serious trouble. . . .

He used the *kyrios*, which means "mister," and the *kyria*—"mistress"—constantly, as everybody does in Greece. In the office I was always the "Kyria Eleni" and my husband was the "Kyrios Costas."

We kept silent and let him talk away. We were getting angrier every minute, but we tried to keep our tempers. It was only when the two proceeded, half-spent cigarettes dangling from their lips, to go to the bedrooms and open wardrobes and start pawing at my clothes and sniffing at bottles and pots that the officer in my husband exploded. He gave them an icy dressing down that took them unawares and very nearly resulted in a fight. I did my best to calm them, as the last thing I wanted was to see my husband beaten up by these worthy representatives of the new "law and order," but they had been badly shaken, and they decided to go, muttering vague threats. They had been insulted while they were exercising their duty, and they would report it to their superiors. Before going, they asked if they could have a kitchen chair for the guard to sit on. They took it, collected their loot, and went away with dark faces, banging the door behind them.

We heard the scraping of the chair as the man sat on it heavily, leaning his back on our door; then the lift came up and took the other two men down.

We went into the kitchen and made coffee.

Cups in hand we returned to the living room, sat down, and looked at each other. We could not but smile at the incredible sight of the two of us, respectable over-fifties, bullied and locked up in our own house. We fought instinctive movements toward the telephone (after trying it once and finding it, as ex-

pected, dead); we started to speak and stopped in mid-
sentence, realizing that the simplest plans like "We must tell
mother . . . I had those papers to sign . . . The children
were coming for lunch . . ." had developed into complex
problems or impossibilities. We had gone to bed the night before with the prospect of a full day ahead. At this time, this
very morning, I was supposed to be giving a television interview to a team from NBC which had made the trip from New
York for that purpose.

Maybe that was the reason for the "silencing operation"?

We heard the back door open, the one that led directly to
the kitchen, and saw with relief that the maid had been allowed to come. She was a brave young thing, a gay Greek
islander, completely oblivious of anything but the fact that we
had not had any breakfast.

Also she brought us news.

Masses of journalists, Greek and foreign, were all over
Mourouzi Street, asking questions of the guard posted outside
the main entrance of the house. He did not tell them anything,
and he did not look as if he knew much. His duty was to ask
all those who came into the house where they were going, and
if they said they wanted to come up to us at the sixth floor, to
tell them it was forbidden. He did not mind if visitors told the
truth or not. If they said they were going to another floor,
stopped the lift, and continued by foot to the sixth, then the
other guard posted outside the door of our flat was there to
stop them. Also the "television people" had come, a whole
team of them, and they had made a big fuss and had insisted on
being allowed to come up, and only when they were told they
would all be arrested had they stopped shouting. Now they
were taking photos of the guard and the penthouse from the
opposite pavement. The neighborhood knew by now of the

Kyria Eleni's arrest, but nobody really worried very much, because everybody was sure that she would surely be let out tomorrow or the day after.

"And now you don't need *that* suitcase anymore," the maid stated with satisfaction. "Can I empty it?"

The small suitcase which I had kept handy since the first days of the coup had been her constant worry. She knew that I had prepared it for the eventuality of sudden arrest, exile, or prison, and she considered that it was just courting bad luck. "One must not even think of such things," she muttered darkly every time she saw me changing its contents, as spring grew into summer and summer passed into autumn. I filled it with disreputable but practical clothes, pants and sweaters, with a blanket and a small pillow, aspirin, alcohol, soap, and toilet paper, an electric torch, paper and pencils, small quantities of tea, coffee, sugar. And one or two books—detective stories or science fiction—which I usually read when short of anything else and had to replace. I toyed with the suitcase, sometimes putting in a small chessboard, sometimes a mini-radio or a pack of playing cards, trying to visualize my needs in improbable situations. Once I even packed a wig, as a basic element of disguise.

Now the maid took the case away and emptied it with apparent satisfaction.

Meanwhile Costa had dressed and was ready to go out. We were not at all sure how the situation was going to develop, and he had to hurry and give instructions to our solicitor and to our financial manager. We had to think of the children, of the rest of a very large and very dependent family, and of the staff still working on different jobs in the offices. The machinery had to be looked after, the warehouses guarded, the offices cleaned, and the financial department had a full job paying out compensations, indemnities, legal costs.

The children, two big sons from my husband's first marriage, were the least of our problems. Dimitri, twenty-one, and Stephen, twenty, were both students at the University, and they were exceptionally healthy, well-balanced, big, handsome, fair-haired boys, quite capable of handling any situation. They still lived with their mother and their two young half sisters, and refused to take anything in life as seriously as we would have wished them to.

We had, of course, taken most necessary measures long ago, signed affidavits, given detailed instructions, but there were always problems that cropped up day by day. And we were still keeping four houses going: the *Kathimerini* building, the Mourouzi flat, a villa on Mykonos, and a country house in Pendeli, in the northern part of Attica.

Costa dressed quickly and was allowed to go out. He disappeared for two hours, came back for a quick lunch, and decided to go out again. He got as far as the front door.

"New orders—" announced the outside guard. "The Kyrios Loundras also is under arrest. No one goes out."

Probably the report of Costa's "insolent behavior" of this morning had reached the authorities. We just guessed, and we were left guessing. No charge was ever made, and no reason justifying either my own or my husband's arrest was ever relayed to us or to our lawyer. We just had the word of the guard. Both the Kyrios and the Kyria were to stay locked in.

That, then, was that. We were in, the whole world was out, and the city of Athens was just a view.

There is a strangeness about the condition of house arrest that is extremely difficult to define. One easily imagines prison, having read innumerable descriptions and seen photographs and films of every kind of cell, from the dungeons in medieval castles to the electrically operated metal doors of the modern penitentiary. But house arrest, in your own home, is a situation that brings to mind that special kind of nightmare which I suppose most people must have experienced. You believe yourself awake, and you decide to perform a simple familiar act, open a door or lift the telephone receiver, and you find it impossible. An invisible force, a sort of woolly paralysis, is holding you back, and soon terror creeps in and you try to cry out and call for help but again you cannot make yourself heard; and eventually you wake up all wrapped up in a muffled agony.

It is the sudden and complete change of your way of life, combined with the fact that nothing at all has changed in your surroundings, that gives the situation that quality of unreality. Here you are in your own room, with all the furniture and the pictures and the books in their proper places. You look outside the window and there is the same view of the same street in the same city. Life all around you is going on just as usual; you can see the streets full of people and cars; the families in the neighboring houses are living the same life they were living yesterday. Here they are, watering the plants on the balconies, looking out, coming and going, here is one getting in his car, here is the young mother getting the pram out. And right in the heart of your own house the grinding noise on the lift on its vertical route reminds you of the comings up and the goings down of all the other tenants. Nothing has happened to anyone else.

And nothing really tragic has happened to you. Nothing tangible, no sickness, no accident, no misfortune of any kind. And in an illogical way, this makes the isolation more difficult to support. One is conditioned to expect all sorts of miseries from a stay in the hospital or, worse still, from a time in jail;

one accepts that a minor car crash can result in weeks of pain and agony, or that a microbe invading your system can condemn you to the severest isolation. The consequences of these events, however hard to bear, have a sort of inevitability, are a part of the process of living, and they are usually cushioned by the ritual consolations of the ever-present chorus of relatives and friends reciting the familiar "time will heal" routine or the infuriating "it could be worse," which, so long as you are alive to hear it, is undeniably correct. But in your own house, on an ordinary-seeming day, all you are conditioned to accept is normal freedom.

But reviewing the situation, we had to acknowledge that indeed it could have been worse. It could have been far worse if we had been arrested, put in prison, or isolated at home immediately after the coup. We would have missed the chance to speak out and to go on providing an uncensored daily information service to every visitor who came to the offices of the *Kathimerini*. When we stopped all our publications on the day of the coup, we expected to share reprisals together with all the other resisters. We expected to be considered as enemies, and we were quite bewildered when we found ourselves treated as if we were some sort of eccentrics, who sooner or later would come to their senses. The military regime, to its own extreme astonishment and delight, had encountered almost no resistance, even from the ranks of its natural enemies of the left and center left, so that they were not worried by what they believed was a transitory phase, just an exaggerated show of professional respectability.

At first they waited patiently for us to "recover," and during this time we kept open house at the offices on Socrates Street, with most of the staff coming daily to sit around and talk and exchange information, communicating freely with hundreds of people, trying to reach as many people as possible through the spoken word, since the printed one was muzzled. We knew that this phase could not hold forever and that eventually we would be stopped, so we did not miss any opportunity of telling what we knew to be the truth: "The group of officers which has taken over is composed of ambitious fanatics who, if helped and supported, will hang on to power and will inevitably, sooner or later, lead Greece into disaster. Their past, their private lives, their military careers, their words, their actions, leave no margin for doubt or optimism."

As the weeks and the months passed, there came a moment when foreign correspondents started to wonder and even to ask directly how it was that I spoke so freely, how I was allowed to give interviews in the offices of a rebel newspaper, show the empty and silent machine rooms, let them photograph them.

Why was the Junta so tolerant? Just as I was becoming slightly suspect, I was arrested and my name was cleared.

Five months earlier

ATHENS: *April 21, 1967*

It had all started at three o'clock in the morning, April 21, 1967, when Costa burst into my bedroom, put on the light, and told me to get up quickly and dress. Something was happening; he did not know exactly what. About an hour before, tanks and armored cars had appeared on the outskirts of Athens, and now they seemed to be converging on the city. In the news room of the *Kathimerini*, where he had stayed on after I left at about midnight, they had started to get worried telephone calls, not only from individuals, but from ministries, from the police and the broadcasting station. It looked like a military coup of some sort.

A military coup had been one of the ever-troubling possibilities on the Greek horizon for more than two years, but on that night it seemed quite improbable. Nothing that had happened recently could justify it. The last riot, an unimportant, routine affair by the Builders' Union, had passed unnoticed about ten days ago, the Government was in the hands of the Conservative Party, there had been no trouble of any kind to suggest that the Army could have been provoked into action. Only three hours ago, driving from the newspaper toward the flat, I had passed cafés and restaurants in full swing, in a nor-

mal springtime Athenian atmosphere. What could have provoked a crisis in such a short lapse of time?

But when we came down and looked at the street, we realized immediately that something was happening, and
happening fast. The whole mood of the city had changed.
Armed soldiers and officers had appeared, and they formed
cordons, stopping cars and pedestrians. Armored cars were
pouring into the central streets, filling the night with metallic,
clanging echoes. Angry civilians were getting involved in
noisy incidents, and drivers suddenly confronted with closed
streets were sounding their horns in strident chorus. Harsh,
brief commands given by the military were interrupted by
shrill voices asking what it was all about. There was an oddity
in this change in the character of the familiar city noises. Everything sounded wrong and artificial, as if the sound track of
a war film had got itself mixed up with a documentary of
night life in a peaceful city.

We saw tanks, heavy, ambling monsters covered with mud,
take up positions in front of the Ministry of Foreign Affairs,
and soldiers jump from the turrets and go straight toward the
policeman who was standing at the entrance and take over his
place.

"Are they Greek . . . ?" I asked my husband, idiotically.

"Of course they are Greek," he answered. "What else can
they be?"

Of course?

Greek tanks, Greek armored cars, with Greek officers,
Greek soldiers taking over the peaceful capital of the country,
pushing aside the police, pointing their guns at unarmed civilians, looking as if they were getting ready for an improbable
battle against an invisible enemy?

We managed to get through Omonia Square just in time,

and found the offices of the newspaper in a turmoil. The news was now arriving fast, and it was as bad as could be. A strong military force using regular army tanks and armored cars had already taken over all the nerve centers of the city, surrounded the Royal Palace, the broadcasting station, the central telephone offices, and the ministries. The police, taken by surprise, did not take part in the operations, but did not resist in the face of what looked like some kind of action taken by the legitimate Greek Army. Members of the Canellopoulos Government had been arrested, as well as politicians of all parties. The King's whereabouts were unknown.

Nobody had the faintest idea of who could be at the head of the coup. The rapidity of the whole operation had been quite fantastic; in less than two hours a city of two million people had been paralyzed, bound, and gagged.

And no one had been aware of what was coming until it was too late. The Government and the Palace, the regular Army and the police, the embassies and the news agencies had all been confident that there was no cause for any anxiety, and had closed shop or gone to sleep without misgivings. In the newspaper, only three hours ago, we had been at pains to find a suitable front-page story for next morning's *Kathimerini*. And during that time, a small rebel mechanized army had been closing in, ready to take over a country peacefully asleep. We felt guilty that during these crucial hours we had not had at least a premonition.

We sat in my office waiting for the situation to develop. News was filtering through, brought by reporters who had been on night duty and who had collected bits and pieces of information. We prepared a last-minute edition, with a one-column report on our front page. We did not expect to circulate, but we made the change out of habit, in spite of still having little to say. We had the names of some arrested politicians, but this only added to the confusion because they ranged from the extreme left to the extreme right.

And then we heard that the Prime Minister, Panayotis Canellopoulos, had been arrested. We did not believe it until one of our reporters, who took in his stride any amount of violence that could qualify as news, came in pale and shaken and described the scene. He had witnessed it, together with hundreds of others. The Greek Premier lived in a modest four-room flat in Xenokratous Street, a stone's throw from Kolonaki Square, and when armored cars were seen blocking all the roads leading to his flat, word went around that something important was happening. How important and how horrifying the crowd of onlookers did not realize until they saw Canellopoulos being carried out bodily by two officers and heard him shout at the top of his voice, "You are traitors! You are all traitors!"

"After they had gone," the reporter continued, "poor Mrs. Canellopoulos came down in tears and told us what had happened. They had heard ringings and bangings at the outside door, and before they had had time to spring out of bed, an officer was inside their bedroom telling the Premier in hurried but respectful tones that his life was in danger, that they had been sent to protect him, and that he must dress and follow them immediately. Canellopoulos went directly to the telephone to ring the Chief of Police but the officer stopped him, telling him that he must hurry. The Premier had realized that something was seriously wrong, and he went to his study to telephone the King. But by then the officers were getting impatient, and they just tore out the telephone wires. Then he ran back to his room, took out a revolver he always kept near him, and threatened to kill himself with it. But they disarmed him and once again assured him that they were only thinking of his safety, and begged him to agree to go voluntarily. He then said, 'I agree, but upon one condition. I will ride in my own car, and you will drive behind.' They pretended to accept, waited for him to dress, and the moment he stepped out of the house they pounced on him, twisted his arm, and bundled him bodily away . . ."

We heard the story, appalled.

What kind of people could treat Panayotis Canellopoulos in this way? A man who was not only the lawful Prime Minister of the country, but a politician of uncontested integrity and distinction, and a right-wing leader always on the best of terms with the Army?

"I will tell you what kind of people," said one of our older editors thoughtfully. "Extreme right-wing officers. No one else. Mark my words: this is the work of a group which must have decided to take power quite a while ago. And I will give you one name I'm sure will be in it. A relative, a Cretan officer called Stelios Pattakos. I could never get on with that man. He is a brigadier in the Tank Corps. He used to visit us when his fellow officers were being tried for taking part in the left-wing Aspida plot, and he bragged about ill-treating them and putting Papaterpos into a cell three foot square where he couldn't even sit down. I can hear him saying, 'I have a wife and two daughters, and also my neck to think of . . . If we see danger, we will take over, whether the King agrees or not. . . .' "

"But what danger is there now?"

The question was put in unison by a group of far from naïve Athenian journalists who had seen at other times real danger coming from all kinds of enemies. If the coup had come as such a complete surprise to the whole of the Greek establishment, if the Government, the Palace, the police, the news agencies, the Greek press had been dozing peacefully during these past hours, it was precisely because no serious threat of any disturbance, no fear of any imminent danger, was present on the Greek horizon. We had seen storms piling up in the past, we knew the signs, and we would have taken very seriously any threat of a Communist uprising. But if that threat had existed, it would have been visible. It had been both visible and audible for months before it erupted in terrifying brutality in December 1944.

"What frightens the extreme right-wing officers," our editor continued, "can be put in one word: elections. The forthcoming elections must be the reason for this coup. There can be no other. These officers are terrified of a victory for the Center Union. Their fears are not national or political, but purely personal. They know that if Papandreou's lot gets in, they've had it." And we all agreed that if the officers who had been thrown in jail for having taken part in a left-wing plot were amnestied, the right-wingers would very probably be charged as being involved in a right-wing plot. They could now be trying, therefore, to save their skins, their uniforms, and their stripes.

We continued our discussion all through those grey hours of the dawn, and though we had so little to go on, we came up with most of the right answers. It is true that we had been dreading a military coup of some sort. We had been constantly worried by the echoes, the rumors, the gossipy information about unrest in the Army, about the dissatisfaction of the senior officers and their preoccupation with political matters.

The editor who knew Pattakos said: "You don't know these military types. I do. Most of them have been dreaming of power all their lives. They are bitter and ignorant men, reared in a life of poverty and mediocrity. Don't forget that the boy who is sent to be fed and clothed and educated by the Army is, with very few exceptions, the unloved boy of a poor family. He is forced into a career that allows few dreams. He can't hope to become rich and powerful, to enjoy modern life, fast cars, fun, or glory. And the old glamour of the uniform is past and forgotten even in the small towns and villages. The military have been living on the fringe of society as a sort of 'khaki proletariat,' and like all proletariats, they have been preparing a revolution."

Yes, we had realized the danger, but as happens so often in life we had not seen what we could do to avert it. We had talked about the disastrous results which any kind of military intervention would have for Greece, and we had written about it as well. In my own personal column I had repeatedly voiced my anxiety. Just one year before the coup I was writing on *Kathimerini's* front page: ". . . It is incredible that there are people in Greece who precisely through fear of dangers imaginary or otherwise crave to live under the rule of tyranny. To speak of a semi-dictatorship, or a temporary dictatorship, or a benevolent dictatorship of the right, is just nonsense. There is only one man who approaches happiness: a free man. There is only one country that offers it: a free country."

But this kind of catastrophe, although it can be feared, cannot always be prevented, because no one wholly believes in its reality until it actually happens.

Thirty years ago, when the threat of approaching disaster was darkening the horizon of Europe, innumerable important and clear-sighted people read the signals and interpreted them correctly—and what good did that do? And how often in daily life does one not see the signs of an inevitable tragic ending to a drama brewing among one's friends, a divorce or even suicide, without being able to stop the process? It is very nearly impossible to convince anyone that the normal sequence of the future will be disrupted until it is, and then it is too late.

I had talked about this threat from the Army privately, and

17

at length, with King Constantine. He was aware of it and spoke to me with distaste of the various military men who at every crisis hinted at the possibility of unconstitutional solutions of the national problems. He was quite genuinely attached to democratic ideas, and quite clear-minded about what any kind of military take-over would mean for himself. I remember, word for word, King Constantine asking me in rhetorical style: "If any kind of dictatorship prevails . . . I ask you! who would be the first victim? Who else but the King? Who else but me?"

The younger members of the staff, who had lived through nothing more exciting than changes of government and elections and had never endured anything remotely resembling a dictatorship, or known censorship, were plaguing the veteran editors with questions. Past chapters of *Kathimerini* history were revived. The smashing and burning of the first offices in Academy Street, in the early twenties; the closing down by dictators Pangalos and Plastiras; the suffocating period of the Metaxas dictatorship; the seizure by the Germans in the forties; the near destruction by the Communists in the December riots of 1944. An older editor said: "In about two or three hours an officer will come and will ask to see you."
"What for?"
"What for? To give you orders . . ."
Then and there, we decided that this time we would not accept orders. It was not a difficult decision to take. We had often thought and spoken about it, taking for granted that any dictatorship of any political hue would inevitably establish censorship. If our fears were realized, we had decided to stop all our publications. We had told our solicitor about it and had given him detailed instructions as to how he should proceed if we were unable to communicate. We had also decided not to

commit ourselves to any plans or investments that could tie us up financially, and not to buy any printing machinery, until the future looked brighter. We knew that we were crippling the rising circulation of the afternoon paper, *Messimvrini*, by not printing more copies, and we had to deal with constant complaints from all our dealers and suffer pressing offers from the representatives of all the printing and machinery firms. They had laughed when I told them again and again, "I am not buying any presses until I am quite sure that we are safe from the Army."

Well, now some kind of "army" had arrived, and if it came to give us the kind of orders we were expecting, then we knew what we were going to do.

"If you can avoid publishing, do so at any price," another experienced, middle-aged journalist now said, very seriously. "I have lived through it and believe me, for the kind of newspapers we publish, it is hell. Without freedom, we make no sense. If this situation develops into a dictatorship, military or civilian, do your utmost to stop the papers. Any sacrifice is worth it."

We reassured him. Neither my husband nor I was young, we had had our share of a rich and adventurous life, we had been more than satisfied in our careers and ambitions. Costa had been an outstanding officer during the war, and he had left the Navy when the fighting against the Italians, the Germans, and the Communists was over. He then came to help me direct what was an important and respectable publishing establishment. He had no reason in the world to work under humiliating conditions, and neither had I.

In these early hours of April 21, talking quietly, we were feeling uncertain about the future but certain about our own moves. We had taken all the decisions, we had realized all the implications, we were ready to accept all the penalties.

Daylight came, and we looked out of our windows on a city at war. Armored cars and tanks were stationed at the crossroads of Socrates Street and St. Constantine Street on our left, and at Piraeus Street on our right. Helmeted men popped in and out of their turrets, and soldiers with guns and bayonets were patrolling the deserted streets. White-clad nurses were leaning out of the windows of the Polyclinic Hospital, just fifty feet away from us, and tourists staying in the nearby Minos Hotel emerged on their balconies, took a look at the unexpected sight, and quickly disappeared again. There was very little noise, no shooting, and the city, mystified more than terrified, was waiting for the radio to wake up as usual at six o'clock and explain the situation.

All through the night the foreign stations had been broadcasting indifferent news bulletins, ignorant that the most sensational coup in postwar Europe was already hours old. The agencies, Associated Press, United Press, Reuter's, Agence France Presse, DPA, had never realized that they had been without any contact with the Greek capital since two o'clock in the morning. That also was one of the wonders of the night. No one in any of the world's cities, in any of hundreds of agencies, had even by chance tried to communicate with the Greek capital. Just like us, they had been not only without any information, but also without any uneasiness or premonition, satisfied that Athens was sleeping through its normal, peaceful night.

The National Broadcasting Station gave no sound at six, but half an hour later we heard a squeak that developed into a military march. It was the "Army Station," which had started its morning program.

It felt quite unreal, sitting there waiting, silent and tense, to learn what kind of life we would be living from now on, what kind of people would be in the government, what kind of government they would inflict on us.

A solemn masculine voice boomed: "Athens calling. Central Radio Station of the Greek Armed Forces. In a few minutes you will hear an important announcement."

After another military march he came on the air again.

"Because of an abnormal situation that developed after midnight endangering the internal security of the country, the Army has taken over the government of the country. . . ."

That announcement did not throw much light. But the next installment did:

"In accordance with Article 91 of the Constitution, and following the recommendation of the Government, Articles 5, 6, 8, 10, 11, 12, 14, 18, 20, 95, and 97 of the present Constitution are suspended throughout the country in view of the manifest internal threat to the country's public order and security. The Minister of the Interior will publish and implement this Decree. Given in Athens this day, April 21, 1967. Signed: Constantine, King of the Hellenes; The Prime Minister; and the Members of the Cabinet."

"This is a fake! . . ." The chorus of immediate disbelief filled the room. It was not difficult to recognize the blatant lies and discrepancies of the announcement. The members of the Government who were supposed to have "recommended" the suspension of all these Articles of the Constitution had been arrested, and certainly the brutally treated and abducted Prime Minister had never signed this decree. A colossal bluff was on the way, and there did not seem to be any possibility of stopping it. The first announcements were repeated again and again, and then the voice changed and we had further enlightening news.

"By order of the revolutionary committee: *One:* Arrest and imprisonment of any person is permitted without observation of any procedure, that is, without warrant from the relevant authority and without the person's having to be caught red-handed; the duration of detention of an arrested person is not subject to any restriction. *Two:* Release on bail for political crimes is forbidden, and there is no limit to duration of detention pending trial for such crimes. *Three:* Any person, irrespective of his calling, may be brought to trial before special courts, that is, courts-martial or special magistrates courts. *Four:* Any gathering or meeting, indoors or outdoors, is prohibited. Any such gathering will be dissolved by force. *Five:* The setting up of any association with trade union aims is prohibited; strikes are completely forbidden. *Six:* Searches are permitted at any time during the day or the night without any restrictions whatsoever in private homes, public shops, and civilian public service establishments. *Seven:* The announcement or publication of reports in any manner whatsoever, including the press, radio, or television, without prior censorship is prohibited. *Eight:* Letters and every other form of dispatch are subject to censorship. *Nine:* Felonies, political crimes, and crimes of any other type, whether they affect private life or not, as well as those which fall under the jurisdiction of courts of appeal, are to be tried without discrimination by special courts-martial. *Ten:* Any civilian committing a punishable offense, even if it is not directed against the security of the Armed Forces of the State, is subject to the jurisdiction of these special courts-martial. . . ."

Well, now we knew. There was no ambiguity in Order Number Seven. There was no doubt about the kind of government we were heading for. If these announcements were characteristic, we could expect the worst possible kind of military dictatorship.

The speaker continued, tearing the Constitution to shreds, announcing the articles that were being suspended, giving orders to the civilian population to stay indoors, repeating over and over again what we, at least, knew definitely to be a bluff.

There had been no danger "known to the Government." No one had asked the Army to interfere, and, if we did not know at that hour about King Constantine, we knew about his Prime Minister. He had not signed any paper, document, or proclamation. They were lying unashamedly, to keep the country and the rest of the Army under the impression that there had been danger, and to give the world at large some justification for the take-over.

We waited to hear the name of the "Chief of the Armed Forces," and we also waited for the officer who, according to our experienced Athenian journalist, would be coming at any moment now.

But the morning dragged on and there were no new developments. On the other hand we had visitors who, through back doors and back alleys, had managed to get through. A young doctor from the Red Cross First Aid Station nearby had been on duty all night. "We have had many casualties," he said, "most of them from bayonet wounds, also a man from the Telephone Company, a middle-aged employee who was brought in in very bad shape. He wouldn't let the soldiers take over his department, and they hit him with the butts of their rifles."

"Any dead?"

"Only one. He died on arrival. A young man of seventeen. He didn't stop when he was told to. Either he didn't hear or he didn't understand. Then, it seems, the officer in command gave the order to a soldier to shoot, and the soldier shot and killed him. No, I don't remember his name. . . ."

A good friend and colleague, a correspondent for foreign papers, came, went, and came again, keeping us supplied with the reactions of other journalists he had contacted. They all knew that we were being fed with big fat lies, that no member of the Government had had any notion of any impending danger, and that the police had had no information whatsoever about any unrest of any kind in any part of Greece.

A photographer brought exciting news. He had seen the King in the vicinity of the Royal Palace, walking between two generals, looking very pale. He was going to the Palace's Chancellery to get in touch with his counselor, Bitsios, but he had not found him there. Arnaoutis was in the hands of the military. He had been one of the first to be arrested. He had resisted and was badly beaten up. This last incident made us more certain than ever that King Constantine was innocent of any knowledge of the coup. Michael Arnaoutis, a handsome, austere-looking Air Force officer, had scarcely left the King's side for the last eleven years. He had been first his instructor, then his aide-de-camp, then his private secretary, and always his best and most faithful friend.

At that time, around midday, we began hoping again. The radio repeated the same announcements, the coup was still anonymous, and its eventual failure could easily be covered up. Not one recognizable voice had been heard; no one, military or civilian, official or unofficial, could be considered responsible; there had not been any important clash; all the arrests had been made with comparative ease and had encountered a minimum of resistance. Nothing seemed irrevocable—until five o'clock that same afternoon.

Then, suddenly, we were showered with bad news. The new Government had been formed and was to be sworn in by the King at seven o'clock, with Constantine Kollias, Public Prosecutor of the Supreme Court, as Prime Minister, and General Spandidakis as Deputy Prime Minister. The other names would be announced later. Exhausted by the long hours of waiting, by lack of sleep, and by a feeling of calamity, we accepted the disaster as a fact. Something like the first faint, nearly painless sting in a woman's breast was throwing us into a silent panic. Greece was in for a new tragic crisis. Would it be a curable one? Should we ever see the end of it? Meanwhile the radio was setting the mood by playing only military marches and a potpourri of syrupy, sentimental popular music of more than thirty years ago: times which probably, in the minds of these military, were considered to be the "good old days": the days when other dictators prepared other wars.

The sun had set, darkness was falling, and now shots were heard all over the city. The prohibition on circulation of cars and pedestrians had been enforced by the radio announcement that anyone seen in the streets after dark would be shot on sight. We could see the officers standing in the turrets of the tanks, aiming at the sky and shooting, presumably to remind people of the order.

A little later we saw an extraordinary scene which, without the actors' being aware, was played entirely for our benefit.

"Look! They are tearing the Lambraki offices apart!"

We put out all the lights and stood behind the windows. The offices of the Lambraki Youth Organization, a left-wing group, occupied the whole fifth floor of the building opposite *Kathimerini*, at exactly the same level as the one my office was on. As the street was very narrow, we saw the whole show as though we were sitting in the front row of a theater. Under the glaring lights, soldiers, officers, plainclothesmen, and regular police were invading the rooms in a frenzy of haste, rushing in and out, taking away ledgers and books and files, at the same time assaulting with rage all the inanimate objects they found in their way. Desks and chairs were banged about as if they were human, the walls were ripped open, the curtains slashed, crockery and ashtrays were smashed on the floor, all with a fury that was frightening to see.

We drew the curtains, put on the light, sat back, and waited.

Not for long. At twenty minutes past eight, after the National Anthem, we heard that the new Government had been sworn in in the presence of the King. Three new names had been added to the two already announced: a Colonel George Papadopoulos, another Colonel Nikolaos Makarezos, and Brigadier Stylianos Pattakos. The first name brought to our memory an unsavory story of a framed sabotage some years ago. The second name no one had ever heard before, and what we had heard this very morning was our only knowledge of the third, Pattakos. We expected the King to speak, but it was Kollias who was heard.

"The Communists were threatening the country; the Army has had to intervene. . . ."

Prime Minister Constantine Kollias repeated what he knew to be a lie to Greece and to the world, forfeiting in those few minutes a whole respectable past. We waited for some words from the King, but he did not speak. I was to be the first to hear him, in a few minutes' time.

After twenty hours of silence the ringing of the telephone in an office along the corridor made us jump as if a bomb had exploded. I lifted the receiver on my desk and, miraculously, it gave a friendly, familiar purr. It worked. Communication was again possible.

In one last desperate fit of optimism, I dialed the number of the King's secretary, to ask whether the King had been present, whether he had *really* sworn in that new Government.

At the other end of the wire a well-known, high-pitched voice answered me directly. "Who is calling?" . . . It was King Constantine himself, and it was his first call, also, as most of the Palace telephones had been disconnected. In a sudden feeling for secrecy we spoke in English. I asked him if it was true that he had sworn in the new Government. Yes, it was true. He had agreed to swear in the Government. He could not do otherwise.

"I have found myself completely isolated. Completely alone."

We talked for a little longer. There was not much to say. I just tried to warn him against future collaboration.

"Don't associate; don't talk to them; don't let yourself be photographed with them. Stay away."

He agreed, but his young voice sounded desperately tired.

There were only two other people in my office at that moment, my husband and P. Lambrias, the editor of the *Messimvrini*. They had guessed that I had been speaking to the King, but still they asked: "It was the King . . . ?"

"Oh yes."

We felt genuinely sorry for him. Two years ago he had lost a very wise and loving father. We were quite sure that nothing of this kind could have happened if King Paul had been alive today. All the politicians were engaged in bitter feuds, and the most important one was sulking in Paris. His own counselor had deserted him, the Army had betrayed him. That day he must have confronted, for the first time in his life, insolent stares coming from men dressed in Greek uniforms. He had the right to feel isolated.

That night we slept for a few hours on couches, and when we woke at dawn, we found that the guard had gone and that the tanks and soldiers had disappeared. Timidly, people were coming out of their houses, taking a look at the streets. Soon the first cars were around. On the morning news bulletin, the radio announced that circulation was permitted and communications would be functioning again. We started for home. Influenced by those long hours passed in the company of people who had recognized what had happened as a major catastrophe, we expected to find a city subdued, silent, and sad, if not in angry revolt. But the faces of the people we saw did not register any special emotion, and the shops had opened and were full of customers; cars and buses hurried on their way, voices were raised in loud salutes and exchanges of small talk. A few tanks, peacefully parked outside some public buildings, were the only remnants of the one-day "revolution." Anyone who had no knowledge of the events of the past twenty-four hours could easily have believed that what the town had suffered was nothing more serious than a power shortage of some sort, an electricity failure or a general strike, and that whatever it had been it was now put right again.

No one seemed to realize what had happened: that a visible or invisible occupation force had taken over the country, that the individual had lost in a few hours what he had fought for for centuries and died for in the last war.

The Athenians were hurrying to take up life on this Saturday morning where they had left it on Thursday night. The gap of Friday the twenty-first was put aside.

The porter of our flat greeted us joyfully. "Well now, we are well rid of those stupid elections. . . ."

Returning to the offices after a quick change and an effusive reconciliation with the two deeply offended dachshunds, I found myself surrounded by foreign journalists just arrived from all parts of the world. The airport at Ellinikon had been opened to air traffic since the early morning, and planes arrived one after the other, filled to capacity with newspaper-men, photographers, radio and television teams sent to report on the coup. They thought that they had arrived to witness the beginning of a long and bitter struggle, and they could not believe that the initial fight, the photogenic one with the city filled with tanks, armored cars, and soldiers, and empty of all civilian presence, had disappeared in the early morning. The night's work had been perfectly timed, admirably well executed, and of a lightning rapidity; but the next day the shrugging indifference of the population of Athens helped it more than military efficiency had done. The people in the streets did not show any kind of concern, did not seem to care one way or the other. It was not a victory for anybody, man or party, it was an all-around defeat for all politicians of all de-nominations, a philosophically accepted overthrow of a situa-tion that evidently did not appeal to the majority. "Let them have a go," was the feeling of the day.

We tried to explain to the foreign correspondents what we ourselves were at pains to understand. We knew that thousands of Communists and important politicians or leaders of the left and left of center, had been rounded up during the night, and that thousands of others were probably now in hiding. But Athens is a city of two million people. And if we were to be-lieve that at least half of them were ready to vote for Papan-dreou in a few weeks' time, that they were liberal and progressive and champions of democracy, where were they?

In the past weeks they had been ready to flare up in vocifer-ous indignation at the idea that just one article of the Constitu-tion, their beloved 114, was not sufficiently respected. Only a few days ago thousands of students, workers, builders, mem-bers of Workers' Unions marched through the streets of Ath-ens, voicing their devotion to democracy and their readiness to fight on its behalf. And now, today, there was not a sign, not a whisper of any anger or bitterness, no reaction of any kind, no protest, nothing. The photographers and TV men roamed in vain over the city to find traces of "the revolution that was," and they inevitably ended up in the offices of the Greek newspapers.

"Who are those people? Why the coup? What is going to happen now? Is the King with them or against them? How is it that there is no resistance?"

While the foreign correspondents were learning who these people were, so were we, by piecing together particles of information collected from officers who had at some time or other met them in the Army. The result was not encouraging. Papadopoulos was the one best known, and he had an all-around bad reputation as being morally and physically unhealthy. He was nicknamed "Nasser" in the Army, had been involved in an unsavory story of sabotage frame-up, and was considered a neurotic who had secretly been undergoing psychiatric treatment. Pattakos was vaguely remembered as a martinet and a religious fanatic, and as for Makarezos, he could have been the original invisible man so little was his presence remembered by anybody. They all had undistinguished military careers, but they were all considered loyal to the throne and staunch anticommunists. That was the reason why they had been placed in top security positions, a misjudgment that had allowed them to bring off the coup. There was no question of their having been called by anybody to save Greece "from imminent danger," as no one was aware either of danger or of their existence.

Meanwhile, the question was, what would the *Kathimerini* do? It was Saturday, and normally we should be on the way to publishing the Sunday edition. All the staff had arrived and sat waiting, at the offices, the news desks, the machine rooms. The whole building, nine stories, three basement and six above ground, was filled up with personnel waiting for orders. There was also a constant shuffle of emissaries between the other newspaper offices, and a counting of casualties. The two left-wing newspapers, *Avghi* and *Allaghi*, had been closed down, and those of their staff who had not been arrested were in hiding. The liberal Center Union *Eleftheria* had lost both publisher and editor-in-chief—the first, Panos Kokkas, had vanished, and the second, George Androulidakis, had been arrested—and the staff had decided to suspend publication. There remained four, *Acropolis* and *Eleftheros Kosmos*, both extreme right-wing, and working furiously to get their Sunday edition ready; the *Vima*, the most important left-of-center pro-Papandreou paper; and the *Kathimerini*. If there was one paper that would refuse to surrender to the new state of affairs, the guess was that it would be *Vima*.

But it soon became evident that *Vima* was dutifully getting ready to send the Sunday edition to the censors, while the *Kathimerini*, surprisingly, was not. A brief visit to our offices was sufficient to prove that nobody was working, that all the editors, employees, visitors were talking, smoking, drinking coffee or ouzo, answering telephones, seemingly waiting for some further instructions.

"You have only to send two copies of each page to the Press Ministry and two to the police . . . ," anxious advertisers told us repeatedly. They were doing the round of the newspapers to learn the fate of their insertions.

It soon transpired that we did not like the situation and that we were sitting back until it improved, and our stand was immediately criticized. Friendly ambassadors were sent to visit us. Didn't we realize that it was uncomradely not to publish? If other newspapers were accepting the situation, a much more painful one from their political standpoint, if the *Vima* was publishing, why did we show such sensitivity? The technical

Constantine Kontos, the writer's maternal grandfather, an eminent scholar and professor of Ancient Greek.

Angelos Vlachos, paternal grandfather, diplomat, poet, and translator of Shakespeare, Goethe, Racine.

New York, 1947. Eleanor Roosevelt entertains George Vlachos and his daughter Helen at a luncheon at the United Nations.

George Vlachos, son of a distinguished Athenian family, emerged very young as a brilliant journalist, a career that did not prevent his being very much a man of the world. He brought many fine qualities and a deep love of life to the *Kathimerini*, in which, as publisher and editor, he had scope to express himself as a fighter and a crusader.

Hollywood, 1939. In the Metro-Goldwyn-Mayer studios, the writer interviews Clark Gable between takes of *Gone with the Wind*.

difficulties of producing the four-page newspaper that the circumstances allowed were negligible, and surely the military would treat the *Kathimerini* with special courtesy.

We offered no explanations, closed offices, gave the staff leave until Monday, and went out of Athens to our house in Pendeli. Experience had taught us our lesson. During the last war, when the Germans entered Athens, they came to the offices of the *Kathimerini* and made the offer to buy the newspaper, title and all. This they did to all the important Greek newspapers, and they were accepted by some. My father, George Vlachos, then publisher and editor, not only refused, but rather naïvely announced his decision to stop publication. Next day a three-man committee, two Germans and a Greek, took over, and a list of the names of those whose access to the offices in Socrates Street was forbidden was pasted on the front door. We headed the list, my father and I, and many of the staff were equally summarily fired. Later they appointed an editor, a poor middle-aged Greek collaborator, an alcoholic named Travlos, who published for a time a pale phantom of a newspaper. We had had nothing to do with the *Kathimerini* all during the war, but still we would have been much happier if we had found a way to stop its publication.

This time we knew better. Unless we could publish a respectable newspaper, a newspaper that was free to inform and not obliged to misinform, we would not publish anything at all. But we were not going to advertise our decision.

Next day, a Sunday, three morning papers appeared, the two of the extreme right, *Acropolis* and *Eleftheros Kosmos*, and the center-left *Vima*. They were identical, with the same headlines, the same official announcements, and the same commentaries. They were not only mutilated, but forcibly fed with lies and poisonous barrack-style propaganda. They were sickening to see, and they dispelled our last doubts.

There was no question, under those conditions, of publishing the two newspapers.

Meanwhile the absence of the Sunday *Kathimerini* from the newstands had made quite an impact—but not of the kind we had hoped. Our readers were simply annoyed at what they considered a lack of publishing efficiency. If the others had managed to publish their newspapers even at such short notice, why couldn't we do as well?

We did not come back to the offices at all on Sunday, and that resulted in the nonappearance on Monday of the afternoon paper, the *Messimvrini*. And this time the outcry was angrier. The *Messimvrini* was a comparatively young newspaper, launched just six years ago, but its rise had been meteoric, and its public was composed mostly of young people, faithful and fanatical. We had hoped that they would understand and appreciate the reason for the paper's disappearance, but there again we were mistaken. They were definitely unsympathetic. They too were quite sure that if we wanted to we could persuade the Colonels to let us publish the *Messimvrini* just as it was before the coup.

Only inside the offices at Socrates Street did we feel at home anymore, especially as we had the satisfaction of seeing the majority of our staff wholeheartedly supporting the decision not to publish under the present circumstances. From colleagues working on the other Greek papers they were hearing fantastic stories of incidents between harassed editors and stubborn military censors. "We cannot print this headline in the size you have ordered."—"Why?" roared the censor. "We told you, we can't fit it in. We can't squeeze the type. We print an eight-column page. We'd have to add two more columns to our width. . . ." The leading articles were sent from the Ministry, the layout ordered by a brigadier, the titles and the size of the type chosen by the censors, and various orders from anonymous officials poured in by telephone. Someone remembered the old fascist principle: "In a well-censored press everything that is not forbidden is obligatory."

Among the first handouts sent from the Ministry with the mention "obligatory" were a succession of articles, leaders, and features, all denouncing the overthrown Government as "corrupt." That is a practice common to all military regimes, white, black, or yellow, communist or fascist, and the most easily accepted by the majority of the people. That we had our quota of dishonest politicians no one would care to deny, but it was more than unjust to underline corruption in relation to the Canellopoulos Government. Not only was it composed of the best elements of the Conservative Party, most of whom were of indisputable integrity, but it had been in existence less than a month. It had not even had the time to be corrupt. The handouts also made much of the country's being "sick," and in this they were right. What they did not realize was that they, the military, were part of the sickness, and that they had now erupted in Greece's life more like a rash than a revolution.

During the first days, we never stopped trying to unravel the tangled whys and hows that had brought about the disaster, feeling all the time that it was a job for the future historian, that time was needed to put the responsibilities in the right perspective. Who had been more to blame, who had finally allowed, or helped, the *ante-portas* military to reach their goal and take over from the politicians? The short-sighted Palace counselors, the loud-mouthed and irresponsible members of Parliament, shouting revolutionary slogans in unashamed demagogy, the section of the press that not only reported them but magnified them, the whipped-up warnings of "Communist danger"—always a useful preelection vote-winner for the parties of the right, in which we had also indulged—or were the CIA and the Americans the real culprits?

Among the journalists, as well as in the group of politicians, writers, or just friends who were frequent visitors in our offices, there had been little talk about secret agents and foreign intelligence services, and no phobia at all about the CIA or any other American organization. In fact, we were genuinely pro-American, believing ourselves very lucky as a small and isolated nation to have the help and support of this great democratic power. And quite sincerely, in these early hours of the Junta coup, not only did we not accept it as an American-conceived plan, but we expected a violent reaction against it from the American government. But it did not take us long to realize that the American Embassy in Athens, reflecting faithfully as always the feelings of Washington, was showing a tolerant friendliness toward these men who had been guilty literally of having hijacked the country, using the arms NATO had confided to them to protect Greece from real danger. No sign of the slightest democratic displeasure was given, and a press attaché of the American Embassy who had visited the *Kathimerini* seemed rather puzzled at our reactions.

"With the kind of references these men have," we finished by asking him, "do you think they could get a job in an important American firm? Would the Hilton Hotel accept Papadopoulos as a director? And Brigadier Pattakos, what job would they entrust to him? What other but to dress him up with uniform and medals and give him a big umbrella and send him to open car doors? Do you consider Greece so unimportant as to let her be governed by mediocrities who know as little of running a country as they do of directing a hotel?"

We got smiles, but no answers.

We could not understand the Americans, and we could not understand what silenced many Greeks whom we believed to be sincere democrats. We did not want to think it was fear. We had lived through the German occupation with all its horrors, with the daily roundup of hostages, executions, and Gestapo activity, and at that time there had always been resistance in the air. There had been writings on the walls; there had been opposition voiced or murmured. This time it was different. There was a cowed silence where there was no outright acceptance. The members of the brutally dissolved Parliament of all parties, as well as the ministers of the Canellopoulos Government who had not been arrested, circulated freely in Athens deploring what had happened with the equanimity of professional politicians who have lost an election. From Constantine Karamanlis in Paris not a thing was heard, not even a formal protest at the treatment of Premier Panayotis Canellopoulos, the man who had succeeded him as head of his own now-dissolved party, who was a lifelong colleague and a close relative.

The military, themselves surprised and delighted, fortified their positions without any active interference. In this atmosphere the nonappearance of our two newspapers took on an unexpected importance. There was constant quarreling at the newsstands; the telephone at the offices did not stop ringing; the advertisers were furious; and complaints poured in from all parts of Greece. Why did all the other newspapers circulate and ours not? A little censorship in the right direction wouldn't do us much harm. And anyhow we were on the same side as the Colonels. No?

No.

We were not.

That was the message, and the only way to put it across, the only way to defy censorship and let our opinion filter through, was by refusing to publish, refusing to cooperate, refusing to come to terms. We had not counted on being so conspicuous in our hostility. We had not bargained for such an isolated stand. But there we were, and there we wanted to be.

But that kind of protest, the military Government decided, with reason, could not be allowed to go on, and Brigadier Stylianos Pattakos, Minister of the Interior, who was already publicized as the benevolent and paternal figure of the "revolution," was dispatched to talk to us and bring us back to the right path.

He came on Tuesday the twenty-fifth, just four days after the coup, late in the evening, after ten o'clock, to the Mourouzi flat. In civilian clothes, a straight-backed, stocky man of medium height, he was on his best behavior, kissed hands, smiled widely, accepted his whisky and water with a little military bow.

We were alone, my husband and I, and we tried to get him to answer some of the basic questions. "Why the coup? And why just now? What was the danger? . . ." He raised bushy eyebrows, looked at us with wide-open eyes devoid of any expression, and fed us large portions of gooey platitudes.

Of course there had been danger, great danger, but thanks to merciful God and the invincible Greek Army, everything was safe now. Greece was happy and proud again, the enemy was grounded, the miracle had happened. Now there was only one question on the lips of patriots . . . why do the best and most respected Greek newspapers remain silent? Why don't they join the chorus of enthusiasm and gratitude that is rocking the country?

He did not let us finish a sentence beginning with the word "censorship."

"Censorship? . . . What censorship? . . . There is not going to be any censorship for you. You are good Greeks. You will be allowed to write what you wish. We know that you will write the right things. You will not be treated like others. You will help us, guide us! We will create a new Greece together."

We changed the subject and asked with some diffidence why the "revolution" had used the name of Canellopoulos and of the King. We need not have worried. He was quite undisturbed by any feeling of guilt.

"Of course we had to use the names of members of the Government and of the King! . . . *We had to fool the people and the rest of the Army.* Don't you see? We wanted to keep the King out of it until we were sure of success. But how could we have succeeded if the rest of the people and the Army did not believe that the King was with us? We wanted to save the country without bloodshed, alone. We had planned every move. But I will tell you everything another time, so that you can publish the whole glorious story in our beloved *Kathimerini. . . .*"

We were back where we had started. We were told that we must decide to publish again, and quickly, because people were beginning to wonder, to misunderstand.

A few days later it was Colonel Papadopoulos, Minister of the Presidency, who was sitting in the same room, also with a whisky and water in his hand, and a pale smile on his untidy, easily forgettable face. His approach was more subtle. He understood our feelings and he admired our professional integrity. That having been said, we had already done a lot of damage by not publishing, and also by talking to foreign journalists in ways that could be misunderstood. We accepted his polite understatement and reminded him that he himself had promised to lift censorship, and that we were quite ready to wait until he did so.

"Ah, but no," he insisted. "You must show confidence in the Government and the only way to do that is to publish *before* censorship is lifted. After all, here, now, I give you my word of honor, even of military honor, that the press will be free before the end of the month. So, there should be no more waiting."

People who tell the truth seldom feel the need to dress it up with solemn oaths, and we did not for a moment believe Mr. Papadopoulos.

During the months of May and June there was no easing of censorship on the Government's part. I had two more interviews with Papadopoulos, and the second and last one finished with a scene in classic B-movie style, with him literally snarling: "You know, I can *make* you publish . . . !" It seems that he was constantly teased by his heavy-humored colleagues in the Junta about not being able to impose his will upon a woman. And every time he replied angrily that "The Vlachos newspapers will be on the newsstands, and soon. . . ."

Meanwhile, our employees, who had willingly accepted their dismissal without compensation as a gesture of solidarity with our stand, were called by the Union of Journalists and ordered to sue. When they refused, the Union decided to do so automatically on their behalf. When the court did not accept the right of the Union to proceed alone, our people were called back and told that if they did not comply, their Union cards would be cancelled and they would not be allowed to work on any newspaper or magazine. And still, many refused. Many had means, others had found odd jobs, some were not working, just relying on their pensions.

At the end of July, the "Papaconstantinou intermezzo," together with the lightheartedness that follows the sun-drenched Greek summer, made us believe that the worst was over and that we would be publishing again.

I was in Mykonos, having a look at the abandoned villa,

when the telephone rang and Mr. Papaconstantinou himself, quite excited, told me that he had accepted the Ministry of the Press (which had been constantly offered to him since the first days of the coup) on condition, of course, that the censorship would be lifted and that a new acceptable Press Law would be drafted by him. He wanted me to come back to Athens so that we could talk things over. I did not doubt his word for a moment. An excellent journalist and writer, he had been a contributor to our weekly, *Ikones*, for years and editorial writer for the *Messimvrini* for the last three. He was a distinguished-looking man, lean, white-haired, with cool blue eyes behind his spectacles, deceptively soft-spoken, with a brilliant but virulent pen. In his youth a prominent member of the Greek Communist Party, he had turned violently anticommunist and had been for the last thirty years a champion of democracy and freedom. During the first weeks of the coup, he had wholeheartedly approved of our stand, and once, returning to the office from an interview with Papadopoulos, he had exploded in disgust: "This man makes me vomit . . . !"

I took the first boat back, and I found everyone in the newspaper in a fever of excitement, putting their offices in order, getting ready for work, discussing the best ways of bridging the three months' gap.

The only question was, "When do we start?"

My worry was that as long as there was martial law and a state of siege, what was given one day could be taken back the next. What if the whole operation had been set up only to fool Papaconstantinou and us? To offer us a few days or weeks of freedom and then clamp down censorship again, under any pretext whatever?

The new Minister's first declarations to the press, both Greek and foreign, were confident and to the point: he "was happy to announce that the freedom of the press, which had been provisionally suspended, would be restored shortly." He added that "particular efforts would be made to promote the journalistic profession in Greece." He declared, "I have always been the advocate of freedom, progress, and social justice, and an opponent of totalitarianism, which has caused our country so much suffering." He pledged continued support of these principals.

That same day the newly sworn-in Minister Papaconstantinou came home to the Mourouzi flat to talk things over. It was a beautiful summer evening, with a light breeze traveling from Phaleron over the trees of the Royal Garden, and we sat on the terrace. He looked and sounded quite happy; he was relieved for himself and for his colleagues that this "difficult" situation was coming to an end. He had the draft of the new Press Law very nearly ready, and he could assure me that it would be more than acceptable, even progressive. Together with the publication of the new law, censorship would cease. There was only one little snag. We should start publishing a few—just a few—days before the new law came into force.

"Just a few days," he continued heartily, "because, you see, now that I am Minister of the Press, you can be quite confident that censorship will be abolished. This time it is a certainty, an absolute certainty. I would never have accepted the post otherwise. . . ."

I could not believe my ears. What the newly appointed Minister Papaconstantinou was now proposing was the old Papadopoulos trap. We had talked about it in the *Kathimerini* offices any number of times and had always come to the conclusion that agreeing to publish under censorship even for a single day would be fatal.

"Now the position is quite different," he insisted. "This is a bargain I made with the Colonels. I accepted the post only under the condition that freedom of the press would be restored, and they promised it. Their one and only wish was that I persuade you to give me—not them—that proof of confidence. The whole future of the Greek press now lies in your hands. What I ask you is a momentary, unimportant sacrifice. You know that in *Kathimerini*'s case censorship will be theoretical. . . ." The very words Pattakos had used.

We argued for hours, while the sun was setting on an old friendship. He refused to accept my view that though he himself was in good faith the military certainly were not, and that if they did not keep their word, he could easily resign— while we, very probably, would not even be allowed to close again.

"If the Government has really decided to restore the freedom of the press, what does our publishing before or after, or even not publishing at all, have to do with it?"

But he answered stubbornly: "It has everything to do with it." We were miles apart. He was sincerely, bitterly disappointed, and when he rose to go, his eyes were full of tears of anger and frustration.

The result of my conversation with Papaconstantinou was eagerly awaited by all the staff, but no one was worrying about the turn it would take. In fact I do not think that they quite believed me when I described the disastrous meeting, and they flocked early next morning to visit him in his Ministry. They returned to the offices aghast. They had found a new, unrecognizable person, definitely supporting the Colonels, advising them to stay away from me and to wake up to the "new reality." He told them to stop visiting the offices and to sue me, and he announced that he was preparing to do so himself. Asked about the future new law and the lifting of censorship, he replied that if censorship were not lifted, that if he had in consequence to resign, and if by this crippling of the press they found themselves without work, "it would be all Mrs. Vlachos' fault."

Censorship was not lifted, of course; the new Press Law was never published; Mr. Papaconstantinou did not resign—but he did sue me, and we never met again.

We often talked about him with interest and curiosity. Which was the real man? The young Communist of the thirties; the adult liberal; the man who had publicly disgorged his disgust of the regime, the Colonels, and especially Papadopoulos, and who had been one of the first to congratulate me on the closing of the paper, accepting his dismissal as an "honor" which allowed him to participate in the sacrifice for the freedom of his profession; or this entirely new, illogical, and dour person? What had happened? Had they threatened him, had they some sort of hold on him because of his past? We knew he was not an especially brave man, and we supposed that he could be easily terrorized. In that case his undisputed intelligence and his liberal feelings probably gave way to the weakness of plain fear.

After that incident the last bridges were cut, there were no more approaches from the Government, and the treatment of all the journalists formerly employed by us took a turn for the worse. They were threatened and hounded out of their new jobs, forced to sue and ask for the maximum indemnities.

A great number of these journalists continued to resist, thus demonstrating their support for our stand to the bitter end. Their courageous defiance inspired the most unethical of the Government's orders: all former employees of the Vlachos newspapers were to be deprived of their pensions and redundancy benefits. We then decided to pay these benefits ourselves, voluntarily. And for the first time since the coup, we called the foreign correspondents to the offices of the *Kathimerini* to announce the decision. We circulated a written message which was widely reported in the foreign press. We had had no complaints on that score. The great majority of the foreign correspondents not only followed our battle with the authorities with extreme interest and sympathy, but also showed us a certain protective care, even to toning down what we told them.

It was just by chance that precisely that day an Italian journalist who had never covered the Athenian scene before was passing through, and friends brought him along to the offices. Less well-informed than his colleagues, he found the whole situation both abominable and fascinating. He asked me for a private interview after the conference, and next day he came for more. And on Sunday the twenty-fourth of September, the Italian newspaper *La Stampa* carried a long and lively story written with zest by my interviewer, Giorgio Fattori.

The questions and answers filled nearly a whole page, and they covered a whole range of subjects: personal, professional, political. I had confessed that I was more afraid of my dentist than of Mr. Papadopoulos; I had said that I had met these Colonels and had found them ignorant and mediocre men; and I had set apart Mr. Pattakos, saying that "he is mediocre, too, but plays the clown. . . ."

That "clown" did it.

For months I had been giving interviews to the foreign press, to radio and television, accusing the regime of much more important offenses than being ignorant, mediocre, or even clowns. I had called them dishonest and liars, I had described them as thugs in uniform, I had used a whole collection of unflattering names and painted them in the blackest colors. Why did that "clown" make such an impression? Maybe it was the drop that made the cup overflow; maybe it was that Pattakos, with his large, bland, mask-like face, did look so much like a sinister clown. Not that Pattakos himself did not react the very next day, in his own inimitable style.

"I refuse to help Mrs. Helen Vlachos, the publisher, to become a heroine by unleashing Government sanctions against her for insulting members of the revolutionary Government. I deplore this breach of the elementary rules of social decorum. Mrs. Vlachos' objective is obvious. She is trying to provoke the Government into reacting in order to 'heroize' herself. But I assure her that she has failed. Her punishment will be her own statements, which brand her indelibly, but also evoke contempt and hilarity. . . ."

This text was read on the Greek radio, and duly published in all Athenian newspapers on September 27.

The next day, I was arrested. The charge: having called Mr. Pattakos a clown.

It was around eleven o'clock, and I was sitting behind my desk at the office giving an interview to the correspondent of the Danish newspaper *Dagens Nyheter*, when I realized that a small commotion was taking place outside my door. My secretary came in, looking worried, followed by two dark-clad men. They were obviously ill at ease, they did not like the presence of a visitor, but they ended by showing me their identity cards. They were from the police, and they asked me to accompany them.

I turned to my visitor. "I am sorry I cannot finish the interview. I have to go."

He looked at me, perplexed.

"Why . . . ?"

"Because I am being arrested. You have got youself a scoop."

I took my bag and left him. He was amazed and speechless

—though not for long. On recovering he swiftly quizzed everyone around and rushed to file the story.

I was escorted to a black police car and taken to the building in Academy Street where the Special Court-Martial held its sittings. The authorities received me with extreme politeness and some embarrassment. The Crown Prosecutor who pronounced the charge was a rather shy young man who told me we had met before. I did not remember him; neither did I remember the old General who interrogated me later for more than an hour. He had known my grandfather and my father, and had been reading my column in the *Kathimerini* for the last twenty years. Quite understandably he wanted to patch things up.

"Can't you at least take the 'clown' back . . . ?" he bargained.

I explained to him that I could not take anything back, because it would be publicized as a fit of repentance. And as I would never be allowed to correct that impression, I had to leave the "clown" as it was.

The judge then proceeded to ask me in hushed tones how I thought the Colonels were getting on, whether I saw the situation shaping up more democratically in the near future, how was the health of his old friend Panayotis Canellopoulos and his other old friend, my father-in-law Admiral Loundras. And he finished by confessing that he missed the *Kathimerini* dreadfully.

It did not surprise me that he recommended my release pending trial.

I came out of the building at about three o'clock to find my husband and a whole crowd of Greek and foreign journalists waiting in the blazing sunshine. I had not much to say, except that I did not know the date of the trial, and that I was looking forward to discussing before a court-martial the implications of calling a brigadier a "clown." I was also quite tired and very hungry, and, as they had been waiting for hours, they too were ready for home, lunch, and siesta.

The decision of the military court was to allow me to be free until the day of my trial. This was duly publicized in the Greek press as a gesture of extreme clemency. But the usual pattern of Junta behavior—officially announcing one thing and unofficially doing another—was followed again. Anyone naïve enough to believe what was published in the Greek newspapers would have had some difficulty in understanding how I had been "set free," considering that Mr. Pattakos on behalf of the Government had said I would not be taken any notice of; and why, after I had been granted freedom again by the authorities of the military court on September 27, a few days later, on October 4, without an explanation or order, armed guards were sent—by an unnamed authority—to see that I did not make any use of it. Promises, oaths, assurances, decisions of courts of law, orders of the most highly placed members of the Government, signatures, and contracts: none of these have any meaning whatever under that kind of regime; all are liable to be swept away, at any moment, by an anonymous voice, for an unknown reason. That civilized and cultured people, inside and out of Greece, could accept this form of lawlessness and disorder, and baptize it "law and order" and believe it beneficial in any way, under any circumstances, seemed an astonishing phenomenon. We had forgotten that it was the existence of such blindness in all countries, even in the most democratic ones, that explained the emergence and survival of dictators and totalitarian governments.

We read, in English and American newspapers, articles and

letters by senators, by MPs, by historians, who with a minimum of knowledge of Greek affairs spoke of the previous chaos and of the present order. They would have approved of Hitler's *law*, and Mussolini's *order*, too.

Time to sit and think

It was our third day of house arrest, and we had adjusted the timetable of our new life according to the foreign radio broadcasts we wanted to hear. This was not only because of our interest in world events, but also because we learned all our own personal news via the waves. Our names buzzed in all known languages. We heard different descriptions of the arrest and the search. We heard all about the so-called "roughhouse" my husband had had with the police, and that it was the reason for his subsequent arrest. We also learned that my trial was going to take place on October 25, and that I would be allowed to see my lawyer only twenty-four hours before.

Two small cups of coffee, and the first BBC broadcast in Greek at a quarter to eight, started the day. Costa was the early morning coffee-maker, producing the "medium boiled" we both liked just right, which is quite an art. Connoisseurs of Greek—or Turkish—coffee will tell you that there are one hundred and forty-four different kinds, but for my part I can't distinguish more than about ten varieties. Roughly, what makes the difference is the amount of sugar that is boiled with the coffee, and the time it is left to boil. With Greek coffee you have to decide beforehand whether you want it without sugar, medium, or sweet, and then whether you prefer it light or heavy. That is the delicate part. You have put the little copper pot on the fire or gas filled with water and with the sugar already in. Now you wait until it boils, and swiftly you pour one spoonful of coffee for each cup. If you let it barely take one swift boil, then pour it directly into the little cup, you will produce the "heavy" type, with a pale froth on the surface, peppered with fine coffee powder. The more you let it boil, the lighter it becomes, the froth all but disappears, and it becomes less "eatable" and more drinkable.

We took our little cups in hand, heard the news, and waited for the porter to bring the papers and the maid to arrive. These were the only people allowed to come into the flat through the back door, and then only after a strict examination by the downstairs guard.

But that day nobody came until half-past nine, when we heard a scuffle outside the front door, which had not been opened once since the day before yesterday, and then the bell ringing.

Ringing once, politely.

We had a visitor. When we saw who it was, we were more surprised than pleased. He was a distant relative, a lawyer who from time to time worked at routine jobs in our legal department. We had not asked to see him, and we could not imagine why he had come and why he had been allowed in by the guard.

Well, he was there; so we welcomed him. Another cup of coffee was prepared, cigarettes offered, news exchanged. He told us that all the telephones of the *Kathimerini* had been disconnected the same day as ours had been as a gesture of hostility, since we were anyhow unable to communicate. He told us that the children sent us their love; they had appealed to the guard but they had not been allowed to come. And then, with the small talk spent, the reason for his arrival emerged. He was an emissary. He had an official pass, and he had come to deliver an ultimatum.

"This time," he said in all seriousness, "you must realize that they have made up their minds to oblige you to publish the newspapers. No, let me finish. You must understand that your situation is much worse than you think it to be. In fact it is desperate. . . ."

Seeing that we were looking at him with more amazement than dismay, he really put on an act. Or was he sincere?

"Please, please, believe me! . . . This is not a joke. I have been sent to tell you that if you don't give in, they have decided to . . . eliminate you. For goodness' sake don't smile. You don't know what kind of people they are. They are capable of anything. This is your last chance to make your peace with them. After all, you have made your message clear, the whole world knows what you stand for. Enough is enough. Now it is time to stop."

"But what are they planning to do?"

"What? I will tell you. They are going to isolate you completely. No one will be allowed to come near you. Do you understand? They are going to leave you without food. They will let you starve!"

In unrehearsed unison, we burst out laughing.

"*Don't laugh!* You don't understand. They will stop at nothing to make you publish. I leave you now, and I will come back tomorrow. I beg you, I implore you—try to be reasonable; think of your families. . . ."

At last he left, and we sat back and tried to assess the situation. We could not make up our minds. Had he suddenly gone mad? But he had got past the guard, and, what was more, no one else had appeared since then. As the hours passed in complete solitude and silence, we tried to take this new development seriously, but we simply could not for our lives make ourselves even begin to believe it.

We remembered grim tales of prisoners starved to death. But they were kept chained, in the depths of medieval dungeons, not in a sunny flat in central Athens, surrounded by friends and neighbors. Anyway, Costa, in his new role of commanding officer of a besieged penthouse, ordered a survey of our provisions. We went into the kitchen, emptied all the cabinets, took down everything from the shelves, made a list of the foodstuffs kept in the refrigerator and in the small cellar and, looking at the result, we were more than satisfied.

We had macaroni and rice in quantities sufficient for months, also flour, sugar, and olive oil; we had whisky, ouzo, and a few bottles of champagne; we had quantities of canned foods, soups, milk, juices, sardines, tuna fish, biscuits, fruit salads, some fancy items like pickles and sauces and spread, and also dog food which we hoped we would not finish by sharing with the dachshunds. We were short on eggs, butter, coffee, and we put those aside together with the fresh fruit, vegetables, and bread that would have to be rationed.

In a way Costa was in his element. He was always an excellent organizer, careful of every detail, concentrating on the problem of the moment, important or unimportant. His years in the Navy, first as an active officer and after the war as an instructor at the submarine base of Scaramanga, had shaped his character in many ways.

Often, before starting on a journey, or even a short excursion, I had to stop him practically taking the car apart to inspect every inch of it.

"Look, if anything happens on the way, we will stop, we won't sink."

So during the whole day and part of the night we went on, half in seriousness, half as a joke, playing this game. We even went further in guessing possible threats. "What if they cut off the water supply . . . ?" And we rushed and filled the baths and all the pots and pans we could find.

The next morning the doorbell rang again, and there the lawyer was. We led him to the terrace, as it was a warm, resplendent autumn day.

"We are sorry, but today you get no coffee. We are economizing. . . ."

It did not take him long to accept the fact that his mission had failed. He made a last bid for cooperation, but half-heartedly, and we told him to stop all this nonsense and go, and that we had nothing to say to him except good-bye.

He went, and we never saw him or heard from him again. Nor did we ever learn any more details about his extraordinary mission. Whose idea was it, originally? Or was this ludicrous plan his own? Had he convinced the authorities that, given a little help, he would succeed in persuading us to publish? We never learned the truth, and we never stopped wondering.

Soon afterward the maid arrived, all excuses and indignation. She had been called early yesterday to the police station near her home, had been kept there all day long, and had been asked a lot of foolish questions.

And while we surreptitiously went and emptied the baths, the porter arrived with an armful of newspapers.

These were our best and most precious company. Surprisingly, we were allowed to go on receiving them morning and afternoon just as we had done before our arrest. The kiosk at the corner could provide the newspapers of the free world the very same day they circulated in Paris and London, and the Government, in a clever mood (suggested by the tourist bureaus), did not stop or ban any foreign newspaper or magazine, whatever its contents. The only newspapers not allowed in Greece were the Cypriot ones, as these were published in Greek and could be read by all Greeks as well as by tourists. And they were violently anti-Junta.

I read English and French papers, any number of Sunday papers and weekly magazines, and had a quick look at the savagely censored and propaganda-infested Athenian papers. All my morning was pleasantly filled with reading and with cutting out interesting items to paste in a day-by-day private memo, a personal mini-publication edited for future reference.

I did not really mind being for the first time on the other side of the paper curtain—that is, completely severed from the world of journalism, just a receiver of information, a reader, an audience. In a way I was relieved. I had never expected to be allowed to speak out so freely and for so long, and I had said and repeated ten times over what I had to say. But just for the fun of it, I decided to speak once more, to finish up tidily that period of my journalist's career, by getting a sort of good-bye message and thank you note to the foreign press. I sat down, made a few drafts, and then copied it in classic prison fashion on very thin paper. I got it out, somehow. I was not at all sure that it would reach its final destination, that is, a newspaper of the free world, or whether, having reached it, it would be accepted as authentic and published.

Two days later, I had the greatest satisfaction of my journalistic career.

There it was, published as top story, on *The Observer*'s front page, with an excellent photograph of me, a three-column title, and a most flattering introduction in fourteen-point type. And my message itself, in twelve-point bold:

. . . I wish to express my thanks for the warm support and interest the International Press of the free world has given to the cause of Greece. And also for the sympathy shown to me personally by friends and colleagues. But the principal reason for it is to ask you to convey a message: "DON'T STOP."

Don't stop writing about Greece, don't stop asking why the Greek Government is not keeping its promises. Officially, publicly, repeatedly, they have all declared that some kind of press freedom would be restored *before* the end of the year. And even a pseudo-freedom would help—an arrangement by which the Greek people will not hear all the truth but at least will not be poisoned and doped by massive daily doses of lies and propaganda.

DON'T STOP. . . .

Don't believe for a moment that what the foreign press writes leaves the colonels cool and undisturbed and that they don't care. They care desperately. They publish with grateful delight the smallest crumb of flattery appearing in the most obscure foreign monthly. They care, but they lie about that, too. (They have inspired one more paraphrase of the most quoted saying of the century: "Never have so few traditionally honest men, militaries and jurists, spoken so many lies in so short a time to so many people.")

So, DON'T STOP. . . .

Now unless provoked by new . . . attentions, I will take time to rest, read and write. Thinking I would be stopped much sooner, I have hurriedly repeated ten times over what I had to say. By now, people with sense the world over know what has happened to Greece. And I ask them to worry about it. It may prove contagious. It did, thirty years ago.

HELEN VLACHOU

After thirty years of active journalism, I have never got over the escalation of minor worries that awaits you at every step of

Helen Vlachou smuggles out plea to Press

'Don't stop harassing the colonels'

MRS HELEN VLACHOU, the 55-year-old Greek publisher who has refused to issue her newspapers under conditions of Press censorship, yesterday smuggled out her first message since she was placed under house arrest last week. In defiant language, recalling a famous open letter to Hitler which her father wrote in his newspaper in 1941 when Nazi troops were ready to invade Greece, she calls on the world's Press to keep up its attacks on the military regime in Athens. Her message is addressed to the International Press Institute (in Zurich) via THE OBSERVER :—

Helen Vlachou on the balcony of her Athens penthouse flat, where she has been under house arrest since Wednesday.

Champion Broome breaks leg

EUROPEAN champion David Broome broke a leg at the Horse of the Year Show, Wembley, London, yesterday.

He was thrown by his novice horse Aberlene which crashed into a fence. Broome was due to ride for the British team in the United States and Canada in two weeks' time.

There were upsets in other sport.

SOCCER : Denis Law (Manchester United) and Ian Ure (Arsenal) were sent off eight minutes from the end of a bitter clash at Old Trafford. United won 1-0.

Chelsea—rocked by manager Tommy Docherty's resignation on Friday—crashed 7-0 at Leeds.

Docherty who heard the result while flying home from Hamburg last night, said: 'I was very disappointed for the boys.'

Asked about his future he replied 'I am keeping my plans to myself.' He said he had been to Germany only to see Germany play Yugoslavia.

RACING : Boismoss, 13-1, be-

This letter is not dated, because it was to be mailed to you by friends living out of Greece in the event that I was stopped from expressing myself freely.

By it I wish to express my thanks for the warm support and interest the international Press of the free world has given to the cause of Greece. And also for the sympathy shown to me personally by friends and colleagues. But the principal reason for it is to ask you to convey a message : 'DON'T STOP.'

Don't stop writing about Greece, don't stop asking why the Greek Government is not keeping its promises. Officially, publicly, repeatedly, they have all declared —from the Prime Minister, Mr Kollias, down to the Press Minister, Mr Papaconstantinou—that some kind of Press freedom would be restored, *before* the end of the year. And even a pseudo-freedom would help. An arrangement by which the Greek people will not hear all the truth, but at least will not be poisoned and doped by massive daily doses of lies and propaganda.

'DON'T STOP . . . .'

Don't believe for a moment that what the foreign Press writes leaves the colonels cool and undisturbed, that they don't care. They care desperately. They publish with grateful delight the smallest crumb of flattery

appearing in the most obscure foreign monthly. They care, but they lie about that, too. (They have inspired one more paraphrase on the most quoted saying of the century : 'Never have so few traditionally honest men, military and jurists, spoken so many lies in so short a time to so many people.')

'SO, DON'T STOP.'

Now unless provoked by newer . . . attentions, I will take time to rest, read and write. Thinking I would be stopped much sooner, I have hurriedly repeated 10 times over what I had to say. After all, by now people with sense the world over know what has happened to Greece. And I ask them to worry about it. It may prove contagious. It did 30 years ago.

(signed) HELEN VLACHOU.

PS: Sorry for the typing —for obvious reasons I have typed it myself.

Mrs Vlachou's letter was cabled to the headquarters of the International Press Institute in Zurich last night. Mr Per Monsen, of Norway, Director of the IPI, said :—

It is almost as if we had anticipated this letter ; for the coming issue of the institute's bulletin which we are preparing contains just such an appeal to all our 1,500 members—editors and publishers in five continents. Mrs Vlachou may be sure that we shall do all in our power to support her in her gallant stand.

Bank chief explains workless speech

SIR Leslie O'Brien, Governor of the Bank of England, claimed last night that a speech he had made abroad about unemployment in Britain was being used for political ends.

Sir Leslie, who was speaking at Gatwick Airport on returning from Buenos Aires, was reported to have referred the to Britain's need for a greater pool of unemployment—' a somewhat larger margin of unused capacity and resources' now than in the 1940s and 1950s.

'If I had thought that someone would take part of my speech and use it in this manner which is clearly intended to embarrass the Government I would not have said it,' he claimed.

Left wing Labour MPs are said to be angry at Sir Leslie's remarks.

'If one is not a politician one does not always think of these things. It is obviously being used for political ends, he said last night. Sir Leslie said his speech—to the Anglo-Argentine Chamber of Commerce on Thursday—was not intended to oppose Government policy.

'My speech was to British businessmen 7,000 miles from home. It was intended to explain to them what I think to be Government policy, and to remove from their minds some of the pessimistic and confused notions they may have on policy which I consider to be successful.'

Dismissal ?

Asked about 'unused capacity,' he said: 'What is full employment is something to be defined. Beveridge thought it was three per cent of unemployed. In the years since the war there has been a very much lower margin.

'My understanding is that the Government has accepted that we need a the way, from the moment you get the idea for a story or an article till the time you see it in its definite form printed in the newspaper. It has all the elements of a fight, which starts as soon as you put the "thing"—article, interview, description, review—on paper. From this first stage, you realize that it has a personality of its own. You write it, but it also writes itself. It takes sidetracks you had not thought of, it corrects your memory, influences your opinion. It is your child but it takes many liberties. Then you send it to be set in type, and if you are working on a newspaper you get it back quite soon, in galleys —a stranger with a new air of importance. At this point, you are prone to exaggerate. Either you find it awful and you want to scrap it, or you read it with surprised satisfaction and relish that the world will have the luck to read it tomorrow. And then you will get the first edition. Where is it? What have they done with it?

There it is. Hidden inside a left-hand page. With a nonsensical headline. And no, that is too much! They have cut the last paragraph, the one that gives a meaning to the whole story. And you can see why, with the advertisement underneath set just high enough to amputate your ten crucial lines. Well, that's that. Nobody will understand what you were writing about.

But there is still more to come. No one has noticed the cut. No one, it seems, really reads. What is the use of taking such pains?

But that Sunday evening, looking at the message transformed from a few lines on a bit of paper to a quarter page right now in a million hands, I felt more of a publisher than I ever had when I directed two newspapers. I knew also that it was the silence of the *Kathimerini* and the *Messimvrini* that had given me a voice and the right to speak out. Nothing that I could ever have published could have had the impact of that piece in *The Observer*, because it was taken over by all the important radio stations and broadcast continuously for the next twenty-four hours in innumerable news bulletins.

After that, I really stopped. That is, I decided to do exactly what I said in my letter: rest, read, and write. If this new situation had deprived me of many things, it had at least offered me a rare and precious commodity which I had never enjoyed before in my life, and that was time. I had time to sit and think, and do nothing; I had time to spare, to squander. I reread old, forgotten books, listened to records and tapes without looking at the clock, and I read newspapers and magazines in a leisurely way which I thoroughly enjoyed—though never quite as an ordinary reader, because I could not refrain from taking notes for future use, if and when I would ever publish again.

It filled the hours, but as the days and weeks passed, I found myself increasingly depressed on behalf of the world press. Not that it did not say the right things about the Greek situation. With rare exceptions it took determinedly democratic and anti-Junta attitudes, and commented on what was happening in a satisfactory way; but there was no heart in it. Especially the top group, *The Times* and the *Monde* and the *Neue Zurcher Zeitung* and the *New York Times*—the elite carefully laid each morning on the most unapproachable breakfast tables, with secure entrées in royal palaces, in diplomatic mansions, ministerial homes, tycoons' offices, and secret service bureaus. These papers seemed to share a new, encyclopedic character. They were full of information from all parts of the world, they voiced expected opinions on most important subjects, they were against every form of "badness," violence, corruption, discrimination, dishonesty; but they preached the right things in the way a priest in the pulpit offers a sermon to a group of sinners, and once that duty was done, they seemed to realize they could not do much more about it.

The personal touch, the anger, the necessary repetition, the fire, the *"j'accuse"* involvement of the great journalist or writer, the driving force of a dedicated publisher, were conspicuously absent. There were probably many reasons for this decline, including the immediacy of other means of obtaining information. The loss of what used to be a monopoly has stripped newspapers of a great part of their power. People do not need them to learn the news; by the time they have a newspaper in their hands, they have already been informed by one medium or another about the important events. In the newspapers they read mostly about the secondary happenings: home news and local politics, sport, entertainment, financial and commercial news, literary events, shows, music, art, society, deaths, and marriage—what radio and TV have no space and time for. I gained the impression that the newspaper as a free, intrepid fighter of causes, as a powerful and courageous crusader, was fading away unnoticed.

The men who were getting the top jobs were intelligent, capable, level-headed professionals intent on producing a good paper which would satisfy the public, the advertisers, and the publisher, and not always in that order.

Success or failure in a campaign undertaken was met as though a game had been won or lost, in a sporting spirit. If an important crisis arose, there was full coverage from every possible angle, well-worded statements of opinions, feelings, and fears—and then, duty done, the chapter was closed and another, more recent one, was started.

It seemed to me that it was not only competition from the other forms of mass media that was depriving the great newspapers of their spirit; it was also, I feared, what I called "the

Lord Thomsons": the new breed of publishers, who in a curious way take pride in not influencing their editors, not taking sides in politics, thus inevitably sterilizing and neutralizing the newspapers they own.

I had met the real Lord Thomson in Athens. He had come to the *Kathimerini* for the traditional cup of coffee, and I remember asking him as a joke if he had not a derelict provincial newspaper on the eve of its demise which he would contemplate selling, so that I could announce that I had bought one of Lord Thomson's newspapers. He was amused by the idea, and we had a pleasant time talking about journalism in general. He was quite frank about his restricted interest in political matters, and very proud of the fact that he very rarely intervened in the policy of his newspapers, leaving the responsibility to his editors. Of course, when one gets to be the owner of a score of newspapers scattered all over the world, one cannot get to know enough about the politics of each country to be able to "intervene" usefully. But then, on the other hand, why buy *The Times,* why become the owner of one of the most influential newspapers of the world, if you are not interested in influencing anybody or any situation?

If Lord Thomson had been the owner of *Kathimerini* and I had been only the editor, the odds are that I would not have taken the responsibility of suspending publication because of censorship and that I would not have been ordered to do so by my nonintervening boss.

That I had been warmly congratulated for taking that stand was just good journalistic manners. I began to suspect that the concept "freedom of the press" meant very little anymore in the wake of advancing cynicism. Modern-style publishers certainly did not worry about it. Editors and journalists did, but they could not do much. And the reading public took very little notice, not realizing that it was itself the victim. Somehow through the years, the "power of the press" had taken on a sinister sound, as if it was mostly the power to be indiscreet—vindictive, offensive, unnecessarily revealing, and critical. How often this power has been used to help, to restore justice, to enforce the weak voice of a minority, passes unnoticed. That the freedom of the press is much more precious for the individual than for the publisher, and that the publisher has not much to lose by accepting censorship, is generally ignored. In fact, it is easier and more profitable to publish a censored paper under a dictatorship than a free newspaper in a democracy. People buy censored newspapers because they have to know for safety's sake the new laws and orders, what is allowed and what forbidden, who is in the good graces of a government and who is to be avoided. What they rarely do is buy two newspapers, because they know they will be identical.

I noticed the growth of another disturbing symptom. The Colonels not only censored the Greek newspapers but also succeeded in curtailing most information to the 'free press." Willingly or not, the foreign papers had to give to their readers Greek news as offered by the Colonels and transmitted by the agencies. As time passed and the people of the regime took over all the important posts, most sources of reliable news were silenced, and whatever the Government announced had to be, if not believed, at least acknowledged without proof or possibility of confirmation. And the agencies, who needed technical facilities more than the foreign correspondents did, had to do their best not to antagonize the Government, and so they dutifully filed all the news as given by official sources. "Censorship is lifted," said Minister Papaconstantinou. "Greek newspapers are now free to state their opinions." This news was sent to the newspapers of the world and published by some. But the fact that censorship had *not* been lifted was not given by any agency, and was not published by any paper, because yet another failure to keep a promise was "non-news" and had no reason to be filed.

And yet I knew that these foreign papers were our most important allies—if not the publishers, then the editors and the journalists. Maybe I am biased on this subject, but I see the good journalist as the last of the free adults in this regimented world. The young have a fling at being militant during their student years, but life soon catches up with them and they have to accept the laws and the taboos of whatever job or profession they enter. With specialization making most of them "know more and more about less and less," they necessarily find themselves aware principally of problems of immediate interest. The man with general knowledge, a keen interest in what is going on in the world, who speaks out with the voice of conscience, and knows how to express himself clearly and sharply: that man is likely to be the responsible journalist.

"Do you know that the Greek Government is paying six specialized guards, heavily armed, to sit in eight-hour shifts outside our doors to protect our isolation? That official orders have been given to the Post Office and the Telephone Company not to trouble us? Other people, to get the tranquillity and peace we are being offered *gratis*, have to go to the Himalayas and spend millions. . . ."

The chance for meditating was there, but the moral tranquillity was absent, and my theory was received without smiles. Costa was worrying about his two boys; he was worrying about all the people, family and employees, who depended on us. A skeleton staff was still working in the legal and accounting department of the newspaper, and the machines had to be maintained, the whole plant kept clean and secure. We knew that our people were intelligent and devoted, but we did not know what kind of difficulties they were facing, if they

Costas Loundras, an officer in the Greek Navy, is an ardent sea-lover in and out of uniform. Here he is seen starting on a fishing expedition with his younger son, Stephen, at his side.

Germany, 1953. During a trip on the Rhine, the writer, a guest of the German government, has a talk with President Adenauer.

Top left. After lunch on the terrace of the Mourouzi flat: Sir Alexander Fleming with Mrs. Amalia Voureka (later Lady Fleming), who is holding Vanya; on her left is Constantine Karamanlis, then a minister in the Papagos government.

Top right. Princeton, 1957. J. Robert Oppenheimer, austere and fascinating, reluctantly allows himself to be photographed outside his home.

Melina Mercouri in a rare moment of leisure during the filming of Kazantzakis' *Christ Recrucified* at Aghios Nikolaos, in Crete.

were being interrogated, harried, threatened. We both worried because we did not know how long this period of house arrest would last and into what kind of situation it would develop, and we were also worrying about my coming trial.

We heard through the BBC and Radio Paris that it was set for such and such a date, and the next day we learned that it was postponed without any reason. We heard that at a press conference a spokesman of the Junta had assured the foreign correspondents that "of course Mrs. Vlachos is allowed to see her lawyer . . . ," when that same lawyer had not been allowed even to send papers for us to sign. After that press conference, the lawyer came home and bellowed to the guard that he was supposed to be allowed to see me every day. We heard such fury in his voice as the guard shouldered him toward the lift that we were sure that next day he would be arrested. We also guessed that if there were going to be a trial, it would probably be held in the early morning or late at night, and that we would be summoned at the very last hour in the hope of keeping the foreign press away.

But most of all, Costa, having been an excellent and law-abiding citizen all his life, could not accept the fact that a thug with a pistol in his hand could sit outside his own front door pretending to be the law.

The morning hours were the most difficult. You woke up with a whole new day stretched before you, a day of empty, silent waiting in a formerly friendly flat that was taking on a different character as it lost its ties with the outer world: a flat with doors that did not open and telephones that did not ring.

Not that we had not at one time or another expected to be put under some kind of arrest. But expecting and experiencing are two quite different things, as you discover in every major crisis in life, and nothing that happens to other people ever remotely resembles what happens to yourself. There are situations that are *supposed* to happen only to other people—to people somehow inattentive or unlucky, who should really have known better than to put themselves in the position of being kidnapped by Eskimo gangsters or blackmailed by sham nuns—or shut up as prisoners inside their own house. "This can't be happening to *me!*" is an attitude hard to shake off.

But there were compensations. During these days we had more time than we had ever had to talk, to think back, to try to assess the past, the present, and the future—or, to be more exact, the different futures we had to think of, from the purely personal, financial, and professional, to the future of Greece, and even of the Western world. We had time, we could spend it freely.

For one of these futures I felt optimistic, and that was the long-term future of Greece. I have never stopped feeling that there is something little short of miraculous in the simple survival of the word "Greece" or "Hellas" through twenty-five centuries of wars, foreign occupations, massacres, and catastrophes of all kinds. This survival has been due to the only important product of our barren land: its people. Greece existed and exists because of the Greeks, because of a small, indomitable minority that can always be relied on to emerge from the Greek soil, a golden vein amongst heaps of mud and stone and rubble. That little unknown Greek is our secret weapon. Often he does not look anything much; he is an ugly little devil, with shining eyes, a warm laugh, light on his feet, razor-sharp in his reactions, and with an extraordinary core of courage and grandeur hidden underneath his unprepossessing exterior. He is a born hero without knowing it, and he has always saved Greece from extinction, from assimilation and slavery, the one authentic unknown soldier, fighting, dying, and being born again. It is thanks to him that Greece is not what shows on the maps—a rugged geographical nonentity—but a gem of a small country, an island of western spirit and culture. That this indomitable Greek was not at present visible was not fatal. Maybe he was waiting, maybe he was very tired and bitterly disappointed, and he would let the new masters of the moment, whoever they were—ambitious compatriots or indifferent foreigners—stay in power for a while and believe that they had won the game. Maybe now he was only a little boy and a little girl getting ready for the future fight for freedom, revolution, rebellion that would inevitably explode.

What we could not understand, in all sincerity, was the reason for America's involvement with the present regime. We had tried to keep some doubts during the first days of the coup, but soon after we had to bow to reality. If the Americans had not engineered the coup of April 21, they had frankly and openly supported it ever since. What had made them do it?

One of our most clear-sighted political commentators used to tell us that he was sure that it was a genuine mistake, based on the relative success of a similar experiment in Turkey: a quick take-over by the military, a clean sweep of unwanted politicians, and a return to a more manageable semi-democracy. "When an ant makes a mistake," he used to add, "you don't feel it. But the mistake of an elephant tramples you." And this copying the Turkish blueprint was definitely a giant mistake.

We had talked about it after the coup with many Americans, trying to make them realize that when we insisted that "Greeks are not Turks" we did not always mean it in the way they thought we did. We could not but accept that Turks are better diplomats by far, that they make better chiefs, better governors. The Turks knew how to give orders better than the Greeks, and the Turkish people are infinitely better at obeying them. They have always automatically respected authority, whether represented by a sultan, a president, or a general. To try to create the same political situation using such dissimilar elements was amateurism at its most dangerous. The military group they were helping was neither respected nor willingly obeyed. The people of Greece were despising the regime, mocking it, playing for time; like termites they were gnawing at the bases of the new Greek establishment. What we did not know was how long it would take them to bring it toppling down.

In the intervals of remembering and speculating, we reminded each other that we should be grateful that we had no discomfort to endure, that we should concentrate on keeping calm and fit. Costa was an excellent gymnast, and he continued with his exercises and push-ups while I walked up and down the terrace, a wide, L-shaped strip graced with a breathtaking view.

Athens is a city of many faces. Most of them are commonplace, many are downright ugly, some are charming, and a few are of unsurpassed beauty. One of the choicest was the one offered to the imprisoned inhabitants of the top floor of Mourouzi Street 1.

"What a lovely green city Athens is!" a guest of ours once exclaimed, peering down from the terrace. He was an American journalist who had just arrived from the airport for lunch and had to leave Athens the same day.

"Don't go back and say that," we warned him, "because no one who knows Athens will believe that you have been near the place."

He could not believe that what he saw was really all the green there was, and that in that city of two million inhabitants, this was the one and only real park, called either the "Royal Garden" or the "National Garden," according to whether we were being a monarchy or a republic. Only the narrow street of Herod Atticus separated us from the park railings and the immensely tall and slender cypresses that bordered it, an austere and elegant guard of honor which came right up to the height of our flat, with tapered tops swaying in the lightest breeze, at times gaily alive and noisy with chirrupy sparrows. Beyond, the park spread, thickly planted with trees of all shades of green, obliterating any view of the modern city, allowing a white glistening shoulder of the marble Stadium to show on the far left, while on the right, the soft line of the Parnes Mountains was just discernible on clear days. Between the two, the Bay of Saronikos, a strip of silver-blue sea, provided the ideal backdrop for the square rock, rising in warm-colored nudity, supporting at its center the fragile-looking, miraculously graceful temple. The Acropolis and the Parthenon, the most perfect marriage of a work of nature and a work of man, are a soul-satisfying sight from whatever angle, at whatever hour, drenched in the blazing Athenian sun or stripped of color in a metallic, dreamlike moonlight.

I have tried to photograph some views in my memory, looking at them intently, and then shutting my eyes and recalling them, and blinking again to see if I had got all the details, imitating a camera, hoping to print them in some specially sensitive part of my mind. I have secured a small collection that comes instantly alive, available at any moment, colors bright and shapes distinct. And one of my best-loved is the Acropolis as seen from Mourouzi Street.

Our generation has added reasons to feel grateful for the ancient rock. During the last war it provided us with the best defense weapon in the world. If the long-drawn wail of a siren suddenly shattered the night, most of the people living in Europe would wake with an icy feeling of dread—with the exception of the very young, and of the Athenians.

The sirens made us leap out of bed and run onto the terraces, the roofs, the balconies, wherever we could look at the sky. We knew that we were safe, that no one would dare to drop a bomb near the Acropolis, and we did not want to miss what was very often a unique spectacle. We sat in the dark, our heads covered with helmets or improvised shields for protection from falling shrapnel, and as the humming sound of approaching aircraft drew near, the searchlights began to sweep the skies with long silvery shafts. Up there, free men were alive and fighting. They had come to bomb the port of Piraeus, or German or Italian military installations around the city of Athens, and we wished them luck with all our hearts. Soon the tracer bullets, yellow, red, green, raced up, embroidering the sky with a gay pattern that erupted from antiaircraft guns. Often the aircraft dropped what we called a "Christmas tree"—a Verey light—and for some moments this brilliant chandelier of blinding lights attached to a parachute descended slowly, lazily, to earth, bathing the whole city in a golden glow. The noise grew louder; the dry bangs from the antiaircraft guns, the boom of the heavy artillery, and the crack of pistols being fired at random in every quarter of the city composed a pandemonium which just allowed us to recognize the distant thuds of the bombs as they were dropped on their targets. Often the attacking planes traveled directly over our heads, over the city.

I don't think I shall ever forget one special night when, together with some tens of thousands of other invisible Athenians, we spent some interminable minutes of agonizing suspense. An air raid was on, the searchlights had begun their leisurely perambulations, when all of a sudden they caught a plane, just one solitary plane. In seconds a deadly network of fire was focused on what appeared to be a small, shining, blinded insect, which went on and on, from Kifissia right over our heads, through hell let loose, toward the sea. It flew steadily and we waited for the inevitable sudden flare, followed perhaps by the shadow of a parachute, and all the while an old woman squatting at the corner of the terrace was praying and crossing herself and murmuring aloud: "Send him a little cloud, dear Virgin, a little cloud to hide in. . . ." And still the plane went on. Miraculously it got to the sea and was lost on the horizon.

It had escaped. The searchlights, like disappointed giants, swept the skies once more and then switched off. And suddenly an unexpected sound was heard, a light, gay, incongruous sound of clapping hands. In pitch darkness the city was applauding the small, solitary, unknown hero. He had won his battle, and that night thousands went to bed sharing a feeling of victory.

Yes, then it was war, and we knew what we were fighting for, and whom we were fighting against. Our enemies were not so much countries or people as regimes. It was the Nazis, the Fascists, more than Germany and Italy. Then we were told by our Western allies that we were brave little Greeks, and that our duty was to die "for freedom and democracy."

Now the same allied powers, the same former friends, have changed their tune. What we must be now is patient little Greeks, and not insist too much on the luxury of "freedom and democracy" for ourselves because it does not suit their new strategic interests.

Security had tightened after *The Observer* article, and quite often we could see unknown men strolling in what they believed looked like an absentminded mood on the adjoining terraces.

No visitors were allowed at all, except my mother once, for a short time, but we knew that many tried constantly to get past the guards: journalists, relatives, friends, all without any success.

So when one evening the door bell rang insistently, we guessed, quite rightly, that it would be the police again.

We had learned our lesson from that very first morning, and we did not open the door, but just talked through a small square opening. Two plainclothesmen were standing outside, and they explained that they did not want to get in, they wanted me to get out. They had been sent to take me for questioning to the Police Headquarters in Bouboulinas Street. The Minister of Public Order, Mr. Totomis, was expecting me immediately.

Costa did not even consult me.

"She will do nothing of the kind, not at this hour. Enough is enough. Come tomorrow at a proper time, and with a proper order, and we will see. . . ."

They did not seem to understand.

The Minister had given orders, he was waiting, and I was to go. So please, would I get ready? . . .

When they realized that I had no intention of getting ready, they began to sound ugly.

They had their orders. They were told to take me to headquarters, and they would do so, whether we liked it or not. If necessary they would break the door and take me by force.

Costa closed the small opening in the door and let them shout outside. They were yelling now, all kinds of threats and insults, and banging the door. Then they shouted that they were going to get help and come back to break the door open.

We heard them go down in the lift. I decided to change into street clothes and put a few necessities into a bag, so that I would be ready if things took a really nasty turn. This time, they had us both quite worried. We did not know the reason for this sudden call. And we did not know what exactly was in those memos and letters that the police had taken away the first morning when they searched the house. Jotted names and telephone numbers, often illegible even to me, or forgotten—they could be anything, a distant relative or a recommended plumber. But in the suspicious mind of the Secret Police this kind of irrelevant scribbling can look quite sinister.

We had a long argument, as I insisted that I should accept and go willingly if they came again and really tried to break the door, but Costa was quite adamant. There was no reason in the world to submit to being dragged in the middle of the night to Bouboulinas in the company of two angry thugs. He was confident that they would not risk waking up the whole block of flats, many of them rented to foreign tenants, by first breaking up a solid front door and then a number of inside doors, one after another. At the worst our conduct would get us bad marks and probably prolong the period of detention, but that was unavoidable.

That night we did not sleep.

They kept on coming to the door, ringing, banging, and shouting. The lift was in constant motion, and we strained our ears to hear if they were trying to force the lock. We had put out the lights and spent most of our time at the farthest point of the living room, waiting for developments, and it was only in the early hours of the morning that the comings and goings stopped.

We went to bed quite exhausted, and sure that they would appear next morning, together with the maid, who could not be expected to keep them out. And how objectionable they would be then, we could only guess.

But the next day, on the contrary, brought reassuring news. The maid had been told by the guard that a "gentleman of the

Public Prosecutor's office would come this evening at eight o'clock, to accompany the Kyria to the Ministry and please would she be ready at that hour." We sent an affirmative answer, also through the maid.

It had been our practice since the very first day not to go near the door, not to engage in any small talk with the guards. We left them in complete silence and boredom for their eight-hour uninterrupted shift, sitting on the confined landing between the lift, the staircase, and our door, and we had discouraged the maid's instinctive hospitality and her tendency to offer little snacks and coffee. It was meant to be both offensive and defensive: we did not want familiar exchanges with the police, we wanted to remain silent, invisible, in fact for most of them completely unknown. It could prove, we vaguely thought, somehow useful.

A very respectable middle-aged official, dressed all in black, accompanied by a subdued policeman, came exactly at eight. They were quite polite, they never referred to the previous night's events, and I did not talk about them, either.

It was quite eerie, after weeks of isolation, coming out into the familiar street, conscious that a small group of people had stopped on the pavement and was looking on with curiosity, and that the wife of the porter, a fat, timid woman, was peeping behind the group, smiling tearfully in silent greeting. I looked around hoping to see someone I knew, but it was already dark and near dinner time, and my ride to Bouboulinas was uneventful. We took a lift, arrived at the second floor, were shown to a deserted waiting room, and then we sat on a wooden bench, in silence. Not for long. The Deputy Prosecutor himself accompanied me into the Minister's office, a plain, unprepossessing room with second-rate modern furniture, the portraits of the King and Queen hanging slightly crooked on stained walls, and a bulky desk behind which a rather young, fleshily handsome man was standing. I had never seen Minister Totomis before, and I had never heard of his existence before the coup. He was, it seemed, a card-playing chum of some Junta members, and a frequent escort of the Junta ladies. He had been mobilized during the first days of the coup, when the Colonels had been told to distribute the ministries to civilians, and the only civilians they knew were either relatives or chance acquaintances.

Hovering uncertainly between the parts of a stern Minister of Public Order and a sophisticated man of the world, Mr. Totomis rose, greeted me civilly but unsmilingly, and offered me one of the armchairs that stood in front of his desk.

"I cannot understand, and I will ask you to explain, the reason for which you persist in not publishing your newspapers. You deprive the Greek public, and you put yourself. . . ."

I breathed more freely.

They had not found any suspect or mysterious document; I had not got anybody into trouble; this was not an interrogation, it was just one more chapter of the same old story. As I had not answered that kind of question for more than a month, I was quite ready and willing to explain my idea of what journalism meant, and why I believed that I had the right, if not the duty, to stop producing something which I considered not only unnecessary, but harmful.

We had got to the subject of censorship, and Mr. Totomis looked both severe and interested, when a side door opened and a short, squat man in uniform came in.

The Minister leaped up and stood as much to attention as his civilian appearance would allow, and in a solemn voice introduced me to Mr. Ladas, the General Secretary of the Ministry, whom I knew to be the real boss in the Ministry and a member of the hard core of the Junta.

Mr. Ladas grunted an acknowledgment and went and sat a

little further away on a wooden bench. I had heard quite a lot of stories about him, and an echo of viciousness and brutality had led me to expect a man of some personality. But he was nothing of the sort: he had a pale, square face with blurred features, small, cunning eyes, short, sandy, cropped hair, and sitting with a slight crouch, with his short legs barely touching the floor, he resembled a sickly kind of ape.

He looked up without lifting his head and between two grunts asked me in a rasping voice:

"Why do you hate the military . . . ?"

Hearing these words, I realized that in a moment of fantasy I had decided that he was incapable of human speech. I had never encountered any other human being who embodied the missing link between men and anthropoid so satisfyingly as did our detestable Mr. Ladas. And my deep animal-loving instinct getting the better of me, I replied to him quite nicely:

"But I don't, Mr. Ladas; you are mistaken! I like military men—I am married to an officer."

"You once wrote in the *Kathimerini* against the increase of the officers' pay!"

I had to confess that I did not remember the occurrence or the reason. He did not believe me. If I liked military men, why did I stop the newspapers?

I sat back, lighted a cigarette, and started all over again. But in a few minutes he interrupted me:

"What do you think of Karamanlis? Are you for him?"

"Karamanlis is an old friend. But what is the use of my being for him now? You have the power. If *you* are for him, why don't you call him back?"

"Grrrr. Mmmm. Grrrr."

He suddenly bolted. He did not like the set-up, or the tone of the conversation. After a small pause we took over where

we had left off. What Mr. Totomis wanted to know, or what
he had been asked by the Government to inquire, was under
what conditions I would agree to publish the newspapers
again. What did I really want? Could I tell him?

Certainly. It was quite simple. What I wanted was what the
Government had promised to give. What Prime Minister Kollias and Ministers Papadopoulos, Pattakos, and Papaconstantinou had declared to Greeks and foreigners that they were
ready and willing to offer: a new and acceptable Press Law,
which would tell the publishers what they were *not* allowed to
print.

He looked at me surprised. Was that enough? It was, I explained, because what was unacceptable was not the fact of not
being allowed to print all the truth, but of being obliged to
publish all the propaganda rubbish and lies issued by the Ministry of the Press. Let me have that famous Law, and providing
I was released from house arrest and had the telephone recon-
nected, I could at least start thinking about publishing again.

He pretended to be impressed. He told me that he would go
the very next morning to see the Prime Minister, and repeated
that he considered my stand quite reasonable, though he had to
protest against my characterizing the Press Ministry's releases
in such a harsh way. Anyhow, he did not see any unbridgeable
differences. We were advancing to a complete theoretical solution of all the problems when the side door opened again and a
grunt summoned him to the other office.

He would let me know, he promised, quite soon. He was
sure that any difficulties would be overcome. For everyone's
sake, mine, the public's, the Government's . . .

The same policeman, alone this time, was waiting to accompany me back to Mourouzi Street. My husband was waiting
up, rather worried and very curious.

"I will tell you just this: when I heard Ladas speak, really speak, I wanted to pat his flat head and give him a lump of sugar."

"What are you talking about?"

"Let's have a drink and I will tell you."

After that we waited for Mr. Totomis' message, which never came. He had probably not realized that all this had been discussed long before, and that what the Junta wanted was not a restrained yet independent newspaper, but the *Kathimerini* publishing dutifully all the paranoiac speeches, all the "Christian" messages, all the nauseating barrack-literature produced by the new political elite.

We had to accept that on that question, at least, they had been really sincere. They did want the *Kathimerini* to be published, they did really miss it, they felt that they had not really succeeded without having the *Kathimerini*'s stamp of approval. At first we believed that it was primarily the act of hostility on the part of a conservative establishment that hurt them, but as time passed we realized that they really missed the *Kathimerini* (not the *Messimvrini*, which was too recent and modern-looking). They were more sensitive than we had thought to the fact that the *Kathimerini* had been for the last forty-eight years the newspaper which gave the stamp of respectability to people, to parties, to governments; that, for many people, and for the Colonels, too, apparently, it automatically supported the "good" and condemned the "bad." The *Kathimerini* had supported Papagos and Karamanlis, and they had been young soldiers when the most famous text of modern Greek journalism, the "Open Letter to Hitler," had been published on March 8, 1941.

This inspired and beautifully written article of my father's was reprinted in hundreds of thousands, and is still religiously kept, framed, in innumerable Greek houses. Published in all the newspapers of the allied world, it gave voice to the most courageous decision of the Greek people. This was to fight the Germans after the Italians, if necessary:

. . . It appears—so the world is told by wireless propaganda —that the Germans want to invade Greece. We ask you why. If the operation against Greece was essential to Axis interests from the start, Germans and Italians would have attacked side by side. Why is it so now? It is perhaps to save the Italians in Albania; but would not the Italians be finally and irrevocably defeated the moment even one soldier set foot in Greece? Would not all the world shout that 45,000,-000, after attacking our 8,000,000, were now begging for the help of another 85,000,000 to save them? Perhaps you will say to us, "What about the British?" We reply that we did not bring them. It is the Italians who brought them to Greece. Do you wish us to tell them to go? But to whom? To the living? For we can hardly dispatch the dead, those who fell in our mountains, who landed wounded in Attica, and here breathed their last, those who, while their country was burning, came here and fell here and found tombs here. . . .

. . . Your Excellency, there are some infamies that are not done in Greece. We can send away neither the dead nor the living. Instead we will stand beside them till some ray of light shines again and the storm finally passes. . . .

Small or great, the free army of the Greeks will stand in Thrace as it stood in Epirus. It will fight. It will die there too. In Thrace it will await the return of that runner from Berlin who came five years ago and received the light of Olympia, and has changed it into a bonfire to bring death and destruction to a country small in size but now made great, and which after teaching the world how to live, must now teach the world how to die.

In commenting next day on this letter, *The Times* wrote:

81

The letter which covered the whole of the front page of the *Kathimerini* electrified the public, and all day crowds thronged Constitution Square. Only those attuned to the peculiar instantaneous atmosphere which binds people living at the foot of the Acropolis can divine with what subtle communicative instinct all Athenians knew immediately yesterday that March 8 was a great day in the history of resurgent Hellas.

This day had been *Kathimerini*'s most glorious, but innumerable other days, along with the best-known Greek signatures, had built a solid and glamorous image for the paper. Kazantzakis was *Kathimerini*'s special envoy during the Spanish Civil War; Metaxas (before becoming a dictator) was a regular military contributor; Mirivilis' many novels started as serials written for the *Kathimerini*; and after the war, practically all the important copyrights, Churchill's *Memoirs* included, were offered to the Greek public through the *Kathimerini*'s columns. Sir Alexander Fleming wrote articles expressly for the *Kathimerini* when he came as our guest in October 1952, and on the same occasion decided to crown his romance with the charming Greek scientist, Amalia Voureka, who became Lady Fleming.

The fact was—and we took some time to realize it—that the military did not accept that the *Kathimerini* was private property, that it belonged to, of all people, a woman. Quite sincerely, they contested my right to stop publishing it. It was "their" newspaper, not mine, and I could not deprive them of a lifetime's companion.

In that view, we had discovered to our astonishment, they were supported by a great part of our reading public. Some had swallowed, hook, line, and sinker, the "imminent communist danger" myth and considered our conduct incomprehensible, unpatriotic, and stupidly ruinous. Others did not relish the situation but just missed their familiar newspaper. After all, almost everyone had more or less yielded to the reality of the "revolution," so why did we behave in this slightly freakish manner?

We had met people who had admired our stand, and used to tell us so—unknowns who stopped us in the street and shook our hands on doing the "right thing." But we suspected them of being nonreaders. They admired a disappearance which did not affect them at all.

With so much time on our hands, Costa and I were lucky in that after sixteen years of marriage we still enjoyed each other's company. It had been a second marriage for both of us. My first one was long ago forgotten, lost in prewar times. It was short, childless, pleasant: an undramatic love affair between a charming young man from a good Greek family of Constantinople, Jack Arvanitides, aged twenty-three, and a girl of twenty-one. Our families were against it because we were considered too young, and because the fact that the bridegroom was an exceptional dancer did not reassure them that he would prove to be a good husband. Two years later, when we decided that they had been right, with the usual family contrariness they did not want us to divorce. But we did, and remained friends ever after.

With Costa, it was a different story. An Athenian, born in 1915, one of four children, two girls, two boys, his life had been Navy all along. His father, retired Admiral Dimitri Loundras, had lived all his life either on active service or as head of naval colleges or as Naval Attaché, and Costa had gone directly from primary school to naval college and had graduated just in time to join the war in 1941. He developed into an excellent submarine commander, capable, courageous, and lucky, with an instinct for survival. He was also ideally cast for the part in being the accepted spare, lean, handsome type. Between missions in Alexandria, where he was based, he met and married Elli Cazoulis, a young woman of excellent Greek family. The marriage proved a failure from the very start, but what with the war and the arrival of two boys it was kept going, artificially helped by good manners and good intentions. But there was no happiness and no understanding, and when I first met Costa Loundras in 1947 he was a solitary figure roaming Athens between leaves, and very few people even knew that he was married. He divorced soon after, then his wife married again, and a year later we followed suit.

That year, 1951, was a crucial one in my life for more reasons than one. I married in May, and in August my father died and I took over the *Kathimerini*. Elections were due in September, and they were especially important, as we were the principal supporters of the new coalition of right-wing parties under the name "Greek Rally" and the leadership of General Papagos.

Not that *Kathimerini* was a new burden. Born in 1919, she had always seemed to me like a younger sister and the most important member of the family. Her political influence, daily circulation, neat appearance, and financial health were the principal subjects of conversation and the source of daily worries, as well as of moments of pride and joy. She was the difficult child, which I was not.

During the first years, *Kathimerini* was violent, young, witty, passionately fighting for the return of King Constantine, bitterly anti-Venizelist, with a daily editorial on the front page always written by my father. Printed in heavy bold type, it was eminently readable, in a personal mixture of *kathare-voussa* and *demotiki* (old and modern Greek) which has never been excelled in style and clarity.

The newspaper, and politics, completely disrupted our family life during the twenties, and I was often sent to stay with my grandparents in Socrates Street, which was then a residential house with a courtyard, a well, a garden. There I lived in idleness, spoiled by my grandfather, a patriarchal figure mellowed by the years, and by my grandmother, a plump bundle of cheerfulness nicknamed "Grouly." She was a Cephalonian, born in Manchester—of all places. Her father was a widely traveled merchant, and his children were born all over the world. She had married at sixteen the important Athenian Angelos Vlachos, a writer, poet, and diplomat, and also a widower forty years old. She started very unwisely to produce four daughters one after the other, and that, coupled with the difference in age, never allowed her to feel really familiar with the tall bearded man who was her husband. When at last her fifth child was a son, and her sixth—my father—another, she relaxed and started a gay social life, holding a "literary salon" in Athens, collecting all the poets and writers of the day, but tempting them also to spend night-long sessions of whist and bezique. Not that she ever overcame her dread of Angelos Vlachos, and it was common knowledge that there were two family histories, the one that was told to grandfather with all the happenings expurgated, censored, rearranged, accommodated, and the other, the true one. Grandmother loved having me around, and she was supremely indifferent to schools and lessons, telling my worried mother: "Leave the poor child alone, with her father in prison. . . ." or "in exile," or "just out of prison," or "back from exile," as the situations would arise.

"Wave your hand! . . . Look up. Say hallo to Daddy

. . . !" I remember being told this outside the grim, grey walls of Averoff prison, on the assumption that Daddy was behind one of the windows in a cell somewhere, and that he could see me if I could not see him. That was a natural state of affairs during those tragic years of catastrophic wars and bitter political struggles, and it troubled me very little. I liked staying with my grandparents, I liked the company of grown-ups, I played very seldom with other children, and I loved all animals indiscriminately. The Vlachos family was predominantly cat-loving, but I was a cat and dog lover, and mouse, frog, turkey, donkey . . . every living thing I could get my hands on, big or small, wild or friendly. I was quite a big girl, about eleven, when my parents realized that I had never been to school, and that I was enjoying a Tarzan-like education right in the heart of Athens. The decision was taken to send me out of Greece to a boarding school in Switzerland, but it was also decided that first I needed a period of transition with a good governess.

That brought a Scotswoman called Miss Ann Bridge to our house. She was tall, thin, middle-aged, with pince-nez glasses and a black velvet ribbon dividing a greying fringe from a white head of hair. She looked formidable, but she was delightful. She disregarded completely all the anomalies of our household and fitted into our pattern of life like an old Athenian. When things took a troubled turn she used to hang an enormous Union Jack outside the door of her bedroom inside the house, and as often as not, nobody dared disturb her. She enjoyed teaching and made me enjoy learning; she eased me into the delights of English literature, she taught me games, played chess with me, and helped me to discover new animals to observe. Together we used to take long walks on the rocky bare hills in Attica or near Delphi's ancient ruins and collect docile little emerald serpents.

I was much less happy, two years later, when I found myself at the "Clochettes" in Geneva, a *pensionnat des jeunes filles* of high reputation, and it took me months to get accustomed to the far-from-rigid discipline of the school, and to the food which I found impossibly tasteless. But I liked studying and progressed well in my lessons, and soon I was out of boarding school and in college. As a result, when eventually I came back to Athens, I could not do what I wanted to do, which was to start writing for the *Kathimerini*; I knew excellent French and English, some Italian and German, but very little Greek. Still I insisted on getting some kind of a job, and I was given a minor post in the publicity department.

My ignorance of Greek was considered a family scandal. It was no use reminding them that it was not of my doing. The fact was that I had for grandfathers two of the most learned Greek scholars: Angelos Vlachos, the cosmopolitan who had translated into Greek—and mainly in verse—the principal works of Shakespeare, Goethe, Schiller, Racine, and Voltaire and had compiled the best Greek-French dictionary; and Constantine Kontos, the most famous professor of Ancient Greek of Athens University, a purist who considered Vlachos mundane and very weak on the Ancients. Long before their last two children (my parents) were born, they were quarreling bitterly about everything, even the accentuation of words, and the question whether the word "atmosphere" should be pronounced in Greek "atmósfera" or "atmosféra" was one of the reasons why Angelos Vlachos, on becoming Minister of Education in the Tricoupis Government, sacked Constantine Kontos from his post. This resulted in a student revolt, a "cabal" among the professors, and finally the resignation of Vlachos from the Ministry.

I never knew Grandfather Kontos, who died soon after I was born, but in his portraits he appears as an impressively handsome man, with a flowing white beard. Many stories circulated about his prodigious memory, his library of ten thousand books, all on ancient Greek history and literature, many of them unique and all donated after his death to the Greek National Library, and his defiant paganism (which was severely criticized). It was with extreme reluctance that he had his children baptized, and then with decidedly un-Christian names. I had, on the Kontos side, Aunt Electra, Aunt Olympias, Uncle Leosthenis, and my mother was the rarest name of all, Demareti. Nobody knows to this day who Demareti was, and I doubt whether anybody else except my mother bears her name.

During these years I led a gay and pleasant Athenian life, with my father playing the part of an elder brother and escorting me usually more for his fun than mine. He was much more social than I ever was, and as he was one of the most popular men in Athenian society, he simply basked in the warmth with which he was always greeted. Not very tall but very slim, with brilliant, laughing brown eyes, a clever mouth, a strong nose, a well-formed head with close-cropped, curly, greying hair, and small ears, he had all the marks of a well-bred European. He was a wit and a flirt; he was highly cultured and he had charm: so much charm that he used it unashamedly, frankly, without any restraint. He was not especially good-tempered, but again he had that strange brand of clever and biting bad temper that allows someone to get away with almost anything. He was both insupportable and most willingly supported.

He was not a publisher at heart, nor an editor. He was a fighting, battling journalist who started his own newspaper primarily to be sure that he would have as much space as he wanted to publish his own articles. He very rarely read anybody else's, but if he was conceited as a journalist, he was strangely modest when asked to rise in other spheres. He had opportunities to stand for Parliament and to find himself at the head of the Conservative Party, but he never had any political ambitions. The truth is that he was just a writer, a man of great journalistic talent, with an inexhaustible appetite for enjoying life. He loved the theater, and in his youth he had written a few successful light comedies. Because of this, he accepted the only official position he ever held, and for three years was the Director of the Royal Theater. He was a sincere lover of beauty in all its forms, and an enthusiast, forever curious and interested, never looking back, never referring to the good old days, always awake to whatever today had to give and what tomorrow promised.

Our relationship was extremely agreeable. He loved me very much, and he wanted me to be very happy, but somehow he was never quite certain that I was. First, I was not beautiful, and he could not imagine that a woman could be happy if she was not beautiful. I had to reassure him that I was pleasant-looking enough to have attractive boys around me, and that pleased him momentarily. Secondly, he did not want me to work; not that he was protective and old-fashioned, but because he wanted me to enjoy life as fully as possible, untrammeled by duties and office hours. Even when he was over sixty and I was nearly forty and had been a professional journalist for years, he always wanted me to stop whatever work I was doing, however successfully, and start "enjoying" myself—traveling for pleasure, going places and meeting people, entertaining, dressing up, whatever he believed made women really happy.

It was during my first marriage that I started writing. A six months' voyage in the Far East, India, Japan, China, Indonesia, on the Greek cargo ship *Oros Tavros* of the Kulukundis Company, on which my husband Jack and I were the only passengers, offered so many stories that I had to put them on paper and send them back to the *Kathimerini*. My first article was published in December 1934, introduced with paternal apologies for my deficient Greek.

After that I was hooked. This article and the succeeding ones having been well received, I found myself on my return a roving correspondent, traveling constantly, chasing people and covering events.

In Berlin in 1936 during the Olympics, I met the least impressive of all dictators, Adolf Hitler (in previous years I had known Mustafa Kemal, and he had left me with an indelible impression of fierceness and intelligence), and together with more than a thousand journalists I took part in Mussolini's imperial safari when he inaugurated in triumphant splendor the "Litorannea," the highway that follows the Libyan coastline. Subjects which readers often found more attractive than the heads of states, dictators or not, were nonpolitical personalities who for one reason or another made front-page news. When I wrote back from America, it was not my meeting President Roosevelt in the White House and describing his supremely confident charm that made any impact, but the story of how I was admitted to the sacrosanct set of Metro-Goldwyn-Mayer during the filming of *Gone with the Wind* and had the privilege of meeting two mythical personages rolled into one— Clark Gable as Rhett Butler.

I only stopped newspaper work completely when the Greek-Italian war started. A strong wind of international pessimism had made me take up nursing after 1936, so, being a full-fledged Red Cross nurse, I was immediately sent to a military hospital. I worked with the Red Cross all through the years of German and Italian Occupation, and it was only after the war, in February 1945, when the *Kathimerini* reappeared, that I resumed journalistic work and that I began to write a regular column which I kept on writing without interruption until April 1967. Its form and style were born by chance. One of the first pieces was a reprint of a letter published in *The Times*, which had somehow fallen into my hands. It was entitled "A Yellow Duck" and it said:

Sir,—In a recent issue of *The Times* many parents will have read with concern (if they did not already know it) that "toys are scarce and dear this Christmas" and that "though some are moderately good, others are poor and unlikely to stand up to boisterous treatment, even from a very young child." They will also have noticed a shortage of sweets. To these, as well as to others who earlier in the year suffered from the drought, I commend for their comfort the following narrative of severer privations. It has reached me from a well-known actor in the RNVR, who has changed the part of Hamlet for that of the commander of an unnamed vessel, perhaps H.M.S. *Pinafore*, "somewhere in the Mediterranean."

"My ship's company are busy making toys for Greek children: I've even made a large woolen ball myself, which caused a great deal of amusement among my more masculine friends. We happen to know a wretchedly poor Greek convent, where eighty small children, all orphans, are cared for. The very best that can be done for them is done—but it amounts to practically nothing—they are more than half starved. Many of the babies are red raw—because they have to be washed in sea water, fresh water being so precious that it can only be spared for drinking. None of them has ever known a sweet or seen any sort of toy. The proud possession of the children was a small ring of steel which could be rolled along the floor—not even a tin to beat with a stick—for every tin is required as a cooking utensil, and all sticks are fuel.

"A naval officer I know happened to have a wooden yellow duck on wheels on board—it was an intended Christmas present for a niece in England. He presented it to the

convent. It caused stupefaction! It was received with wide-
eyed silence and gaping mouths—and then solemnly led by
a daring four-year-old out into the street. In absolute silence
all the children followed it, and soon a regular procession was
started, with old men and women, soldiers, priests, everyone—and they all followed the yellow duck through the
main street of the town. Someone found a Union Jack and
hoisted it on a pole. A tattered, dirty drummer appeared
from somewhere, and a fiddler with a squeaky fiddle. They
played, almost unrecognizably, "God Save the King." And
the yellow duck, a hideosity, was finally led, like the Trojan
horse, back into the convent—and so we make toys for them
now and hope to get them to the kids before Christmas."
Your obedient servant,
SYDNEY COCKERELL
Kew, December 17

This "Yellow Duck," enriched with a prologue and an appeal, not only produced a mountain of toys, but also attracted
attention to the new column with the title *Epikaira*, meaning
approximately "of now." As the years passed and it appeared
regularly on the front page of the *Kathimerini*, touching all
subjects and written in very plain Greek, this column secured
for me a definite niche in Greek journalism.

It took me a long time to realize it. Whenever a big story
came my way, and some did, I felt I had to treat it with special
deference, with headlines and bold type and plenty of space.
And when I happened to write about the important people of
the world—Winston Churchill, de Gaulle, Truman, Adenauer
—I again respectfully changed format and even tried to dress
up my Greek. Eventually I had to accept that my short "epikaira" were better liked and remembered, and I finished by
abandoning all other forms of writing and dealt with all subjects, light or serious, in this personal column.

The years to come were difficult and troubled but also in many ways rewarding. The *Kathimerini* had shed all its political fanaticisms and was the top national paper. My father was in a brilliant writing mood, though his health, on the contrary, was failing rapidly. He had had several operations and was constantly in pain. But his mind was clearer and sharper than ever, his interest was alive to everything that was happening around him, he continued to attract the company of politicians, journalists, friends, young and old alike, and both his wit and his charm were intact. Also, with money pouring in from the *Kathimerini*, he indulged in a terrific buying spree. All the financial wounds of the war were healed, new flats were bought and new cars and pieces of land, not counting new machinery and equipment for the newspaper. Thinking back, I get an assortment of conflicting pictures of these first postwar years. I had more and more work in the newspaper as I took over most of my father's duties, I had a lot of writing to do, and I was also the movie critic of the *Kathimerini*. I also got involved in all kinds of different undertakings, successfully launching the "Friends of the Village," an organization aimed to help the war-stricken villages of northern Greece, and unsuccessfully trying as Vice President of the National Broadcasting Service of Greece to give it a more liberal character. It was the one medium of communication in Greece that was always cursed with censorship. Every new government started by promising to free it from the former government's fetters, and finished by imposing its own.

And I shared in the explosion of Athenian gaiety that erupted right in the middle of a chaotic political and national situation: a sort of epidemic of optimism, a spirit of courage and renewal. The country was in real and immediate danger, yet Parliament never ceased functioning, the press was left absolutely free, elections were held supervised by observers sent by the Allies (then democratically minded), and there was no shadow of dictatorship on the horizon.

We were lucky then, because the country was governed by politicians, who even at their worst are better than the military. The military had a war to fight. They were giving battle in the mountains, they were engaged in a bitter, stubborn civil war, they were once again the anonymous heroes throwing away their lives with admirable generosity.

Then they really saved Greece. And the people were at their side, and the Greeks were mature enough to be allowed to hear the bad news as well as the good, without losing faith, without halting the work of reconstruction, without falling into despair, pessimism, or silence.

Thinking back, I realized that I had literally never stopped during the past twenty-two years, my excellent health not even giving me the breathing space of a mild illness. When it was not work or travel or fun, it was the family. As an only child of a clever but doting mother who lived alone and of a demanding father, I was deep in family responsibilities even before I married again and got a husband, and two children, and more family. And as if all that was not sufficient, I had masses of godchildren.

Now there were no musts, no deadlines, no getting up at dawn—together with the *Messimvrini* staff, I had always been at Socrates Street by six in the morning—no house problems, no hairdresser, no social calls, no letters to write, no shopping, no bills to pay, no babies to baptize. That was one of the most consoling thoughts, as baptisms had always been one of my nightmares. Baptizing a Greek child according to our Orthodox rites is a terrifying ordeal to begin with, and one which never comes to an end.

It starts with the religious ceremony. You arrive at the

church bringing new clothes for the baby, a little golden cross, and lots of determined patience. You go and stand near the baptismal font, where the family and the priests gather, and then someone—usually an aunt or a grandmother—arrives with the baby. (The mother, in earlier times, was not allowed anywhere near the church, but now she usually lurks around somewhere.) The ceremony begins with things looking easy and normal. The priest is reading solemnly from a precious-looking book; there is chanting and blessing and praying. But soon dark-clothed women come discreetly with big buckets of hot water and fill up the font, while someone else comes and enrobes you with an enormous cotton apron. Then a big white candle you have been holding is taken away, and the baby is given to you. At this point, the infant is usually just restless, and allows you to go on reciting the Credo, which you are supposed to know by heart, and to speak a ritual dialogue with the priest, during which you reject Satan three times, the last time spitting as politely as you can manage.

And then, in a sudden decisive movement, the priest snatches the baby in strong and practiced hands, divests it of all clothing, and proceeds to drown it in the tepid water. Inevitably hell breaks loose, as once, twice, three times, spluttering and howling, the baby is completely immersed in water, head and all, and is then held up high, a bundle of explosive misery for you to anoint. Olive oil is poured into your palms, and you have to cover the little writhing body completely, touching all the parts, the itching little feet, and inside the ears, and in the openings of the tiny nose and mouth and eyes—and then, as if that were not enough, you have to take a pair of slippery scissors and proceed to cut three little tufts of whatever hair you can discover.

The freshly oiled, desperate, and slippery victim is then deposited in your extended arms. You are agonizingly aware as you clutch it that you will not be able to hold this wriggling bit of humanity for more than ten seconds. Your hands are covered with oil, your apron is wrenched askew, and all the while, a mob of photographers is clicking merrily away, securing for the future revolting pictures of a mad woman criminal trying to smother a baby. Meanwhile, happy and relaxed, the priests, the members of the family, and the crowd enjoy the spectacle. The old women smile with twinkling eyes, make reassuring noises, and clap hands. Only when you have become numb from effort and desperation is the baby taken away, the apron peeled off, and you are free to breathe again: this time, at least, you have not become a murderer. You are then given a piece of soap to wash your hands, and a few moments later the baby, dressed in its new finery but still crying (even if only in a miserable, sniffling, exhuasted way) is presented to you again, as a precious gift. "Its name . . . ?" asks the priest. "She has forgotten . . ." you hear critical whispers behind you. "The name . . . ?" booms the priest. Someone of the family remembers it and you repeat it in shame. And then for years ahead, little girls and little boys arrive at the office or at home, bearing presents, flowers, good wishes on every feast day, name day, or anniversary, either theirs or yours, expecting not only that you will do your corresponding duty, but more important, that you will recognize and distinguish them—a feat rendered the more difficult as they become more unrecognizable with each passing year. The only solution was to photograph them every time, pretending to want the photos as a souvenir, but in reality to keep them in a sort of police file.

I had photos of all my godchildren, and I also had photos of all the major events, travels, meetings in my life. And now at last I had the chance to put a lifetime of photographic chaos into

The principal reception room on the sixth floor of the *Kathimerini*. Portraits of three generations of the Vlachos family adorn the walls: George, his father Angelos, and his grandfather Stavros Vlachos, Minister of Education in the first Greek government after Independence.

Queen Frederica, during a visit to the *Kathimerini*, examines with interest the type being set on the "stone."

Winston Churchill during a luncheon given in his honor at a seaside villa near Sunion. This photo, taken in 1963, shows the great man in an excellent mood on what must have been one of his last public appearances. In the background is his grandson, Winston Churchill.

Alexander Papagos, twice a victorious general and a successful political leader, was a man of extremely simple tastes. He enjoyed nothing so much as a moment of leisure in his modest Ekali villa, in the company of his dog.

some kind of order. I had started photography quite young as an enthusiastic amateur, and I remained one, with just a shade more experience and facility than the normal family snapshot fanatic. I always got a picture, if not the best possible, and I enjoyed all the processes of developing and printing.

Like most photographers, I had tried a variety of cameras, from Rolleis and Contax down to Polaroids, passing through Minox, arriving at prestigious Hasselbladts; and, like most, I had my favorite, the machine with which I felt thoroughly familiar, at ease, and secure, as though it was an extension of my hands, and that was the Leica. I always returned to the Leica, and I had several, and a choice of lenses; the oldest model with a Summitar lens was the one I took if I wanted to be absolutely sure that I would come back with a printable picture.

Now was the time to tackle my photographic past, and I spread boxes and cartons, albums and files and envelopes on the floor of the living room and started sorting them into categories: prints and negatives and transparencies, private and professional, peaceful and wartime, Greece and foreign countries, personalities and events—and animals, generations of cats and dogs.

Costa and I looked at them together. We had met only in 1947, so we had quite a bit of past life which we had not shared, and even after our marriage we were often separated. I had traveled and met people and taken photographs that we had scarcely ever looked at. And many of them brought back a wealth of memories of long-forgotten stories and of faces of people and friends so much younger as to be unrecognizable.

"Is that shy-looking young thing Frederica . . . ?"

Curly-headed and baby-faced, the German bride of Crown Prince Paul had been received in Athens with indifference. She had been born Princess of Hanover in 1917, married in 1938, becoming "Greek" just one year before World War Two crashed into the heart of Europe. She did not at first present any qualities of beauty or personality that could appeal to the Greek people, and she was neither liked nor disliked. She was quiet, young, in love with her husband, and she went on with the important task of producing children, first a girl, Princess Sophia, then a boy, Prince Constantine, then another girl, Princess Irene. Princess Irene was born in South Africa, during the years of war and exile—difficult years through which the young royal couple showed discretion, simplicity, and courage. But no one in Greece expected much of them, and when the plebiscite of 1946 brought royalty back to Greece, Frederica, of all people, passed unnoticed.

Not for long.

It was during these after-war and after-civil-war years that Frederica attained a new stature. I saw her work, and she was magnificent. Her extraordinary dynamism had found an outlet, and she went through the destroyed towns and villages of Greece like a beneficial tornado. She was brave and fearless and full of spirit, she traveled on roads that had proved mined the day before and were to prove it again the day after. She worked for days and weeks and months on end to gather the abandoned children, to find money, homes, help. She created an invaluable organization for the rehabilitation of refugees, she embraced the mothers, she gave shelter to the sick and the incapacitated. She never stopped, she was tireless, she was clever, modern, realistic. She created centers which later became the hearts of the newborn villages. She organized groups of social workers who taught the villagers hygiene, dietetics, farming, weaving.

By the end of the forties, Queen Frederica had gained an amount of recognition, love, and respect that could have lasted her lifetime. She was for a short time in Greek history a unique phenomenon, a well-loved queen; because if most kings of Greece have had their moments of warm popularity, all its queens—Amalia, Olga, Sophia—have been either ignored or disliked.

If only she had stopped then, if she had sat back and taken a well-deserved rest, it is probable that both the history of Greece and that of the Greek monarchy would have been different.

But she did not stop. With the same energy and passionate interest she went into politics. And there also she disregarded the dangers and the loaded minefields.

It was a few days after my father's death that I was summoned to the Palace. Queen Frederica wanted to see me. I guessed that as she had known and appreciated my father, who had been genuinely charmed by her, she wanted to offer personal condolences. I thought the invitation was social, but I soon found out that it was primarily political. I was now at the head of a powerful newspaper, elections were due in a month's time; what was I going to do? Whom was I going to support?

"Papagos, of course. . . ."

I could not understand the question. My father had been trying for years to persuade Papagos to enter politics. We were practically the godfathers of the new coalition of right-wing parties called the "Greek Rally." Who else was there to support?

"You should not do it. You must not help Papagos. He is a dangerous man."

If I had not heard Queen Frederica utter these extraordinary words with my own ears, I would never have believed them. I was completely taken aback, disconcerted. I had arrived at the Palace at five o'clock in the afternoon, and at seven Queen Frederica proposed that we should go and have dinner at the Tatoi Residence, some forty kilometers north of Athens. We went alone in a small red two-seater, an open car which she drove—I don't remember ever seeing her drive again—and after we had had dinner together, we talked until midnight. I was completely mystified. I could not understand the reason for this all-out violent attack against a man who was everything she should have wished for. Papagos was a devoted royalist, a victorious general, a man of austere habits and undisputed integrity, an excellent family man with the most handsome and distinguished wife. He seemed ideal for the post, the answer to any palace's prayer.

During those hours I discovered for the first time the new Frederica—or another facet of an unpredictable woman. She insisted that a Papagos victory would be a disaster for Greece, that I should believe her, that she had her reasons, and that she hoped that I would "obey" her.

That same night, after my return to Athens, I wrote her a long letter. I was appalled, not only by her stand against Papagos, but also by the fact that she was taking the risk of voicing such an opinion openly on the eve of a crucial election. I explained my anxiety and requested another meeting. I sent the letter early in the morning, by hand, to her lady-in-waiting whom I knew personally, and the same afternoon I was again summoned to the Palace.

We talked for three more hours without getting anywhere. Queen Frederica was just as insistent as the day before, she reiterated her "wish and advice" that the *Kathimerini* should not support Papagos, offering vague and unconvincing arguments; and though I tried with "Ma'am's" and "with-due-respect's" to keep the discussion on some level of deference and formality, the fact was that we quarreled bitterly, and when I left, the temperature was at freezing point.

Papagos lost that election, but won with a landslide the one next year. I did not meet Queen Frederica for more than two years, and by that time all was well between the Palace and Prime Minister Papagos. Up to this day I never discovered the reason for this passing enmity, though I often asked Papagos himself. But either out of loyalty or ignorance, he changed the subject or said he could not imagine any reason. Maybe there was no reason, and it was just the fear that a man of acknowledged authority, accustomed to being obeyed, would be difficult to influence. In that Queen Frederica was mistaken, because Papagos never lost his deep respect for royalty and complied with good grace with most of the Palace's wishes.

After that, Queen Frederica began devoting her energy to various social activities, organizing cruises of European royalty through the generosity of Greek shipowners, setting up royal excursions with matrimonial aims, all the while holding onto and administering personally the welfare organizations which had grown out of all proportion and had thousands of employees and budgets of millions of drachmas. Again, I was one of the many who tried to dissuade her from taking that kind of risk, once the war was ended and there was no immediate need. But the slow process of government bureaucracy was intolerable for Queen Frederica, and she was absolutely sure—and there she was probably right—that she got ten times the results working directly, without any supervision, that she would have had if her help had gone through official channels. I believe that on that point she was quite sincere, and that she never realized how vulnerable her position was.

From then on we met quite often. One day I was told that the Queen wanted to go and visit incognito some slums in Drapetsona, in Piraeus, about which she had heard horrifying stories. Could I accompany the Queen there, protect her from being recognized, and present her as a foreign lady, from the Red Cross or something? We would have one policeman in civilian clothes to show us the way. I remember that venture especially well, because it combined both the Fredericas. It started with an unrecognizable woman with dark glasses and a handkerchief tied over her head, immensely interested and genuinely impressed. She was moved to tears by the horrifying poverty, the ugliness, the misery written all over the pale, patient, thin faces of the inhabitants of these caves, relics of the bombardments of the last war. She could not have been more perfect, more understanding, and more warmly human. But after two hours of incognito, she could not bear it. Stealthily she let the handkerchief slip away; then she took off her dark glasses; then she smiled her well-known wide smile. "The Queen . . . It is the Queen . . . !"

We often talked about the Frederica riddle. She had that characteristic German trait of being one day icily formal, and the next embarrassingly familiar.

One afternoon her equerry, Miky Melas, an old friend, came to the office and after some hemming and hawing told me that Queen Frederica had expressed the wish that the ladies who met her should not only salute by curtsying, but should also kiss her hand.

"You come here, to a journalist, to a woman of my age, to tell me that I have to kiss the hand of Frederica? Are you in your right mind . . . ?" He was annoyed, he realized the absurdity of the request, but he could not do anything about it, and rather coldly he told me that he was just a messenger and that if I did not want to kiss the Queen's hand nobody could force me to. I said that I hoped not, and he went away. Of course I never even considered complying with what I really believed to be as silly a "kaiser-like" request as could be retrieved from the well-forgotten past, but the hand-kissing spread and became a "must," not only for all the ladies-in-waiting, but also for the wives of Ministers, and of the officials invited to the Palace, and for the Athenian ladies considered as "friends."

Then, the other facet would come to light. At eight o'clock one morning, a friendly telephone call from the Palace announced that in half an hour Queen Frederica would be at the offices to see the printing of the *Messimvrini*. I tried to persuade her to come the next day, so that the company of journalists, machinists, and typographers would be a little less grubby, but there was nothing doing, and in thirty minutes she was there. We started by welcoming her formally, and we finished by completely succumbing to her easy charm, to her cleverness, to her quick grasp of whatever was explained to her, to her unflagging attention, and to her unexpected lack of any formality.

Painting Queen Frederica either in black colors or in white is just to ignore the complexity and fascination of her personality. Most of her faults sprang from exaggerated virtues, from too much drive, too much initiative, too much interest in what was happening around her, so that she developed into a queen-sized meddler, who could not be stopped or curbed. Also, she loved publicity.

The famous London incident in 1963, which many believe to have started the whole Lambraki tragedy, hit the office early one Monday morning, in the form of a telegram of five hundred words, relating the extraordinary events that had taken place outside Claridge's Hotel. A group of left-wingers had chased and molested the "unprotected" Queen of Greece, obliging her to flee into a side street and demand refuge from an unknown woman. The story seemed too fantastic to be true, and I immediately got into contact with London and spoke with the Queen's acting secretary, Stelios Hourmouzios. He not only confirmed the truth of the story, but he underlined that Queen Frederica had sent it only to me, to offer me a scoop, and that she hoped I would see that it was as sensationally published as possible.

As all editors in the world know, with royalty it is usually the other way around, and it was only because we had genuine doubts about the wisdom of making a splash of a regrettable incident which did little credit to anybody that we did not pounce upon it immediately. When we were told that if we did not want it, others would, we scrapped the whole front page of the first edition of the *Messimvrini* and came out screaming in huge headlines.

Many people believe that Queen Frederica never forgot that episode, never forgave the men and women who chased her; and that she inspired, maybe involuntarily, the roughing-up of Lambraki in Salonika, which resulted in his death: a death that gave birth to a chain of dramatic events. I do not believe that to be true, but the fact is that at the very beginning, the publicity given to the whole minor episode came from anger, from a bitter but unwise wish to make the world know that a queen had been ill-treated. It was not difficult for people to conclude that coupled with anger was a wish for some punishment of the culprits.

By that time, in 1963, Queen Frederica, and I think King Paul, too, had grown rather tired of their Prime Minister, Constantine Karamanlis. They were not the only ones. After General Papagos' death in 1955, the Palace's choice of Karamanlis, up to then only a Minister of Public Works, had been hailed by most people inside and outside Greece as an unexpected success. Karamanlis had done wonders for Greece in many respects. He had proved himself an experienced politician, and he was physically impressive, a tall, handsome man at ease with the people, familiar with every facet of Greek life. He was admired, respected, even loved by the Greek people who saw him fleetingly or from afar. But he had come to be disliked and feared by most of his ministers and his colleagues, and he had discouraged by a mounting stubbornness and extreme aggressiveness most of his supporters and friends. He was, as I suppose many successful politicians are, conceited, completely self-centered, and unburdened by any feeling of gratitude toward anybody. He loved to hear himself speak, and he seldom listened to anyone else. He demanded flattery, resented the slightest criticism, and he inevitably clashed with Queen Frederica who shared many of his faults. Amongst them were a certain disdain for friends, for people considered secure, and a weakness for the unfaithful, as more interesting and worth playing up to. The years of power had been piling up, he had already been eight years in office, and there was a general feeling that an alternative was needed.

Incredibly, and unfortunately for Greece, the two Papandreous, son and father, were chosen for that role. Andreas Papandreou had been invited back to Greece after twenty-five years of self-exile, during which he had become an American citizen, an American professor, with an American wife and children; and George Papandreou, set aside and forgotten for the last twenty years, was suddenly hailed as the "grand old man" of Greek politics. Rested after his long period of comfortable idleness, the older Papandreou emerged as a fascinating figure, an orator of style, using pure Greek to convey beautifully worded political witticisms. That he was a dangerously superficial man, an old-fashioned demagogue, was ignored or disregarded, and two political forces that influenced the Greek scene, the Palace and the American Embassy, began working discreetly together to help the Papandreous.

As the elections of February 16, 1964, were approaching, I found myself involved in a personal controversy with the officials of the Palace, with the King's secretary, Dora Vourloumi, and with the King's counselor, Constantine Hoidas. The subject was King Paul's health. We had reason to believe that the King was dangerously ill, and that the complete secrecy covering this fact did not spring from humanitarian reasons, from the wish to keep the King himself from realizing his condition (he was a man of greater moral courage than he was usually credited with, and deeply religious), but from purely political, electoral reasons.

The Greek people are sensitive, impressionable, and sentimental. Most of them also automatically connect the King, the Palace, and royalty with the Conservative Party. King Paul in consequence must be "for the ERE," led by Panayotis Canellopoulos, and consequently "against" the Papandreous and the Center Union. If the King was dying, there would be many who would not want to embitter his last days by voting for his "enemies." For the less naïve, there was something else which could influence the public toward voting Conservative if they knew the King was in danger. That was the recent death of Sophocles Venizelos. Venizelos, a leading personality of the Center Union, a clever businessman of a politician, a liberal with excellent relations with the Palace, was as good a manipulator in moments of crisis as he was a bridge player—and he was one of the world's acknowledged best. His sudden death during the election campaign left the Papandreous, father and son, without his assuaging influence. And if the King, another man whose quiet wisdom had kept democracy going through the last seventeen troubled years, was to disappear, the feeling was that the gap left in the political scene would rally the people toward the more conservative, safer, right-wing party.

We had the information that the King was gravely ill, but all we got from official sources, even from the caretaker Prime Minster, Mr. Paraskevopoulos, were vehement and aggressive denials. The King was well; the King was better; the King had lumbago—no, the King was suffering from an old ulcer; the King had completely recovered; there was nothing at all, absolutely nothing, the matter with him.

It was on Thursday morning, February 13, three days before the Sunday of the elections, that Constantine Hoidas, the King's counselor, himself telephoned me at the office, and gave me a "tip."

"You are always worrying about His Majesty's health, and you don't believe our words. Well! . . . Send one of your photographers with a car outside the Palace, at eleven o'clock this morning, and he will see the King, who is going for a drive to the sea, and he can follow him and take photographs and show them to you, and persuade you and your readers that the King, thank God, is well, and all the rumors are—well, just rumors!"

We dispatched Vassili, a young photographer who had covered many royal occasions, and waited impatiently to see the results. When he came back and developed the pictures, we had to accept the evidence. The King looked quite well. He had not got out of the car, but he had recognized Vassili, had waved to him, and had smiled quite gaily. Prince Constantine was driving, and Queen Frederica and Queen Helen of Rumania were sitting in the back, and they were all looking happy.

That photograph, exclusive to our papers, was printed next day, Friday, and persuaded many Greeks that the King, if he had ever been seriously ill, was now well on the way to recovery.

One week later, the elections over, the Center Union having carried a majority of 52 percent, a decree was issued giving Crown Prince Constantine the duties of Regent, because of the aggravation of King Paul's serious condition.

HOUSE ARREST

On March 6 King Paul died, just three weeks after his smiling, reassuring photograph.

We remembered together, Costa and I, these bits and pieces of unrelated Greek history, which may have some interest if only because they come from direct knowledge and first-hand impressions. And, hundreds of photographs helping, we also talked about the lighter side of Athenian life.

A lovely profile of Melina Mercouri that I had taken while she was filming *Christ Recrucified* in Crete brought her back to our minds. We often spoke about Melina, not because of her stage and screen career, but because we had known her all our lives, ever since she was a tall, skinny girl with burning eyes. We had seen her burst onto the Athenian social scene and had attended a great many of her performances, both on the stage and off. She had an unquenchable thirst for innocent exhibitionism, she was attractive, tireless, amusing, elegant, and graceful, and she needed a public, always. The theater gave her that public and that is why she adored it, without ever being able to play but just one role, herself. Whenever she was given the opportunity, as she was in *Stella* and *Never on Sunday*, to portray Melina the entertainer, Melina the warmhearted, Melina the infuriating egoist at one moment, but admirably generous the next, Melina the grimacing gargoyle who could transform herself in seconds into a resplendent beauty, she was unique and enchanting. The moment she tried to take on another role, to transform herself into another woman, she lost all talent and all credibility, and no amount of will power and hard work could give her the chameleon quality of the good actress. She could be nothing but Melina, much more "over-Greek" than "over-sexed," trailing a whole tribe of people—family, friends, admirers, hangers-on—so that she could be sure to have her public on hand at every moment of her life.

I had no doubt that her recent awareness of political matters was a direct result of the presence of Jules Dassin in her life. A brilliantly intelligent man, he influenced Melina enormously and gave her much to think about on subjects which had never bothered her before. Not that her hatred for the Colonels was not deep and real. She is a freedom-loving Greek soul, and I am sure that she would have despised a Russian Communist Pattakoff as much as she did our local one; but there again, she was playing a new role that was not quite Melina.

Hers was one successful career. Another friend of past years had a more extraordinary one. Costa had never met Aliki Diplarakos, and I enjoyed telling him her story.

Aliki was the second of four girls of a good but impoverished Athenian family, a dark, raven-haired, classical beauty, slim and straight-backed, a gay young goddess with a ready laugh. Her elder sister Nada, a statuesque blonde, was just as beautiful, but considered colder and cleverer. Without any proof, she is held responsible for Aliki's launching night, an unforgettable Athenian event which I had the luck to witness. The "Miss Greece" yearly contest was on, and at that time it was held in the Olympia theater and was very popular at all levels of society. There was dancing on the circular floor where the stalls had been removed, various turns and the parade of the "beauties" on stage, and an audience composed mostly of elegant Athenians in the surrounding boxes. Amongst them was Aliki, very young, dressed all in white, with a white fox fur stole, and no one to this day knows exactly who looked up at that ravishing vision sitting in semiroyal splendor and cried out: "But *there* is Miss Greece!" The one solitary voice developed into a chorus, the public turned its back on the stage where poor seminaked girls were strutting away, the jury looked at Aliki and melted at the sight, and Aliki was whisked away from her box looking modest, surprised, and unwilling. By then it was too late to be unwilling. Aliki was voted "Miss Greece" by a unanimous popular ballot, probably the only "Miss" to have won a beauty contest without having taken part in it. When a little later Aliki reappeared in her box alone and slowly nodded her head in acceptance, it was not only the crowd which roared its enthusiasm. Even the other "beauties," subdued and overwhelmed by her striking superiority, joined in the applause.

After that night, Aliki and her family never looked back. Aliki went to Paris, won the title of "Miss Europe," and married first a French millionaire whom she divorced after the war, and then a distinguished English diplomat. Nada divorced her Athenian husband and married in France; Edmée and Christine, the two younger sisters (a shade less beautiful), also made excellent marriages; and at a later stage their mother joined the exodus and also remarried. If beauty was the basic ingredient of the success of the Diplarakos family, there were many additional qualities that ensured them an especially popular position, in and out of Greece. This is particularly true of Aliki, now Lady Russell, an indefatigable hostess, a warmhearted friend, always vivid and gay as well as beautiful, who at last count has probably offered more to international society than she has ever taken.

Inevitably, our reminiscing included the Greek shipowners. I know it sounds disrespectful, but I always felt that there was an affinity among royals, shipowners, and gypsies. All are people to be judged, if they have to be judged at all, by a different yardstick from the one used to measure normal people. Because they are not "normal" people.

The "royals," all of them, of any nationality, wherever they may live, are not normal because they themselves, deep inside, believe that they are different. They really and truly feel that they are by birth and blood a superior species of human being. They cannot bring themselves to obey the same rule of law as you and I do, they are members of a tightly knit international caste, and they usually consider marriage to any "royal" foreigner much more suitable than getting involved with a "nonroyal" native.

Going right down the social scale, you find very much the same feelings in gypsies. And somewhere in-between stand the Greek shipowners.

That all three categories are clouded in a sort of romantic atmosphere that keeps the great public magnetized in a state of inexhaustible curiosity cannot be denied. And if the passionate interest in royalty is more understandable, helped as it is by pomp, pageantry, and tradition (and also by the fact that most royals work quite hard at their job, different from other people's as it may be), the interest awakened by the "golden Greeks" is also explicable, being largely due to the exhibitionism of our two feuding giants, Stavros Niarchos and Aris Onassis, who are, in reality, much less typical of their tribe than the world is led to believe.

The average Greek shipowner is a serious businessman, a good *pater familias* living a quiet and discreet life in some capital of the world. He probably comes from Chios, Kassos, or Cephalonia, and he keeps with the island of his birth a sentimental link, which often takes the concrete form of a fleeting visit or a substantial check.

His duties to flag and country end there. Citizens of the world and merchants on the high seas, the majority of our shipowners don't like to share in any sacrifice or take part in any fight that will not bring them material gains. Tax-dodging is a must. Other people may have to pay taxes—may even believe that they gain some strange kind of respectability by doing so—but the Greek shipowner does not believe in sharing his country's or any foreign government's expenses, or in taking part in any country's wars. Whenever the horizon darkens where he happens to live, be it his own country or a country of adoption, he just collects the family and goes to roost wherever it is calm and peaceful and safe. There he finds the other shipowners, and they huddle together for the duration, leading a comfortable bourgeois existence, thinking of ships, money, ships, family, ships. . . . Outside their circle, that urge to add more and bigger ships to their fleets seems a kind of mad collector's mania to have as many huge, rambling toys as possible circling the globe, wearing their names and the names of their mothers, sisters, children. For them, only ships spell success in life. Very few have really beautiful houses, because they don't want to be earthbound; they want to be able, at the first sign of any danger, of rising taxes, or of war, to sail away, find new harbors, go wherever flags are cheap and skies clear.

To criticize them is one thing, to understand them another. They are in reality descendants of the high sea pirates of past centuries (also often represented as romantic cavaliers), and like them, their purpose is to amass as much material wealth as possible so that they can enjoy a comfortable life, buy their way out of every tight corner, keep the family safe and the sons well away from stupid entanglements with dangerous wars.

The females of the species are generally extremely nice women, excellent wives and mothers, and it is chiefly to satisfy their husbands and fathers that they indulge in an amateurish contest of Dior-wearing and Impressionist-buying, with the bulk of growing tonnage faithfully reflected in the growth in karats of the indispensable diamond ring. They have no real social ambition, they live inside their own little communities, visiting each other in their luxurious flats or hotel suites, showing off their children and arranging future marriages based on ships and dowries with the same relish as their island grandmothers. Vaguely religious, more by superstition than from faith, they help in bazaars, buy tickets, dress and show up at all the community's events, and generally behave as they think a good Christian should behave. There are, of course, some families who do not conform to pattern; there are exceptions, usually singled out of the herd, like our two protagonists.

The Onassis versus Niarchos debate is the one topic of conversation that we Athenians share with the rest of the world. The fact that most of us know them personally does not spoil the fun; on the contrary. We can take sides using our own experiences, remembering what happened that day on the *Creole* and how the weekend on the *Christina* developed; that fight during the Carnival; that preelection argument. We can take count of Stavros Niarchos' love affairs and marriages, and Aris Onassis' involvements and social successes.

Both my husband and I knew and liked Stavros much better than Aris. Stavros was an old friend, an Athenian of our generation, and we remembered him since his early years, driving the impressive-looking fast cars of the thirties, chasing the prettiest girls, sailing in increasingly large yachts. Together with our friends we did not believe that he was doing much work in his uncle's Koumandaros mills in Piraeus, but there we were wrong. Not only did he work quite hard, but he also tried to steer the whole family to do what he was doing himself, that is, to invest in ships.

Stavros was clever, quick, decisive, and ambitious. He was also a snob: the best kind of snob. He was attracted to quality, he wanted to enjoy the highest standard of living and to meet the kind of people who knew all about it. Stavros Niarchos was untypical, because his dream of power and riches progressed much further than just ships and plush living and the obsequious smiles of headwaiters in the exclusive nightclubs of the world. He was clever enough to realize that he had a lot to learn about manners, food, art, sport, and clothes. Also at that time, on his way up both in business and society, there was no Onassis on the horizon.

If there had been, I doubt that Stavros would ever have married the ravishingly pretty but penniless and shipless Melpo Kappari. She was a childhood friend of mine, and I followed their courtship, marriage, and divorce closely. Melpo was as near an aristocrat as you can find in Greece, brought up as a spoiled little rich girl before her parents were ruined. She was very small and slim, the *bibelot* type, with an upturned nose, enormous brown melting Greek eyes, a lovely, full, slightly ironic mouth. She was witty, sophisticated, well educated, completely poised, and high-strung. She was also a widow. She had married, at the age of twenty, a handsome Greek diplomat, and together they formed the most enchanting young couple of the Greek Embassy in Rome. They had not been married a year when he contracted a galloping form of polio and died in agony in a few weeks.

I think that Stavros admired Melpo more than he really loved her, and I know that Melpo took quite a time to decide on marriage with that abrupt but overpoweringly generous suitor. When they did marry they had a few happy years, Stavros accepting her condescending ways, and Melpo on her side enjoying the teaching and polishing of an excellent pupil.

But when that stage was over, they started to make each other thoroughly miserable, and they divorced, amicably enough.

That was when a Smyrniot, called Onassis, living in Argentina, was emerging as a new personality in the shipping world. One of his successes was his marriage to Athina Livanos, of the great shipping family, an extremely gay and lovely girl, with a fleet of merchant ships of her own.

Stavros discovered that she had a younger sister, Eugenie, who was just as pretty, and had as many ships. He wooed her, married her, became Onassis' brother-in-law, and the rivalry started. I do not know if Eugenie, a clear-eyed girl with a subdued beauty, loved Stavros when she married him, but I know that she has loved him ever after, and has done so with devotion, dignity, understanding, and infinite patience. Eugenie is the kind of model daughter, model mother, and model wife that is supposed not to exist any more in our wicked modern world. One has only to consider her stand in the Niarchos-Ford crisis, to see that Eugenie behaved instinctively and sincerely like a heroine straight out of a Victorian novel. She helped Stavros to make up his mind and go through their divorce and his remarriage, she protected the four children and kept them as happy as possible, she let the world pity her in silence. This marriage between Stavros Niarchos, an Orthodox, and Catholic Charlotte Ford, after a Mexican divorce, dissolved a few months after the birth of a baby girl. And he returned to Eugenie, as we all knew he would, without having to worry about any formalities. For Greece and the Greek church they had never been divorced, they were as before, man and wife, Mr. and Mrs. Niarchos. In Athens we took this development in our stride. We had never believed the Niarchos-Ford marriage would be a lasting one because we couldn't believe that Stavros would ever leave a woman like

Eugenie for good. But Eugenie herself, sending a husband in his middle fifties into the arms of a glamorous millionaire in her early twenties, could not possibly have been sure what the outcome would be.

Wives, yachts, villas, islands, art collections, were pieces in the game played alongside the more important one of ships, whaling fleets, shipyards, aluminum plants, casinos, airway companies.

My move, your move.

Winston Churchill was traveling on the Onassis yacht, *Christina*, while the King and Queen of Greece were spending the weekend at Niarchos' private island of Spetsopoula, with Greta Garbo thrown in for good measure at the one party, and Herbert von Karajan at the other.

Comparisons being unavoidable, discussion flared over the part of the game we knew more about. I would not accept that there could be any comparison between Niarchos' *Creole* and Onassis' *Christina*. The first was a dream of a three-master, a living ghost from the splendid past, and there was no more beautiful sight on Aegean waters than her, flying past under full sail. There was the sobriety of perfection in her pale ashen teak decks, her warm, gleaming mahoganies, her gay golden brasses. A momentary gaffe of decorating the living room and the cabins with priceless pictures was corrected after Stavros was told that it was a crime to subject them to the salt wind that inevitably blew on them. He replaced them with excellent but not unique works of art.

It is rather interesting to note that no one has worried about the El Greco that adorns the drawing room of Onassis' little floating palace, *Christina*. In that yacht, if everything is not gold, it is certainly gold-plated, and sumptuous enough to satisfy the soul of the most exacting and voluptuous potentate.

The swimming pool on the afterdeck, lined with beautiful mosaic work, not only empties at the flick of a switch, but slowly rises up at another, and at floor level it becomes a gleaming dance floor. Multicolored lights flicker, soft music fills the air, caviar is passed around, champagne bubbles and flows, and Aris Onassis sits down and talks to his guests.

At that point comparisons work the other way around. There is no doubt that the soft-eyed, warm-voiced Anatolian is more interesting, more amusing, more charming than Niarchos can ever be. In fact, Stavros is one of the few genuinely boring clever men that I have ever met. Maybe it is the jarring quality of his voice, maybe his persistent obsession with whatever is his interest of the moment, and his tireless, monotonous repetition of what he has on his mind. He does not really care if you are interested or not in his latest quarrel, his present fight, or his next decision. He takes it for granted that you must be, especially if he considers you an old friend. And he goes on, and on. I can remember evenings in Spetsopoula that could beat in somnolent and respectable boredom any Sunday School gathering: the reality being, I suppose, that Niarchos basically is a serious, solid, responsible man, much more old-fashioned than his fooling around and trying to beat the authentic adventurer, Onassis, allows him to appear.

With Aris Onassis, things were always quite different.

"There is *a* Mr. Onassis at the entrance," a rather diffident secretary would inform me, "and he says he wants to see you. . . ."

"Tell him to come right up."

I did not doubt that it would be Aris Onassis. It was his very clever way to make an immediate and indelible impression on the porter, on the liftman, on anyone who chanced to be around. He tried it every time, and it often worked, as the hall porter did not expect such a humble approach, or simply had never seen him in person and did not recognize him from his photographs.

"Why don't you ring up before coming, like a sensible man?" I would ask him each time. "How did you know I would be here?"

"Well, I would have tried again," he would say, with a slow, pleasant, carpet-vendor's smile, "that is all."

And he would sit and talk and be pleasant, friendly, informative. Also, most of the time, hungry and thirsty. "Do you have any bread and cheese? I am starving."

This, conveyed to the office canteen, created an effusion of hospitality. Whole chunks of cheese arrived accompanied by whatever foodstuffs could be found on the premises, and while members of the staff and visitors came and went, Onassis would munch contentedly, offering the picture of a simple, carefree man, different from those exasperatingly busy magnates, always pressed for time. He wanted to meet everybody, he usually overstayed, as if being inside a real newspaper office was the most exciting thing in the world.

His reason for the visit was sometimes clearly stated, sometimes not even hinted at. It could be just talk, or some information about an accident on the Olympic Airways, or an invitation for an excursion, or just nothing. He felt like coming, and he came, and he always left an excellent impression. Aris Onassis is certainly the top public relations genius in the world, and he concentrates on one client, himself.

His greatest asset is his connections. The rest—houses, art collections, properties—has always been a little nebulous. He has had no real home other than the *Christina*. The other villas, flats, hotel suites were just *pieds-à-terres* necessary for his image and for meeting people on land. He had nothing even approaching the house Stavros Niarchos mounted in Paris, in the lovely quarter of the Marais: the Hotel Chanalleuilles which suffers only from a surplus of perfection, so dressed up with treasures and antiques that it has acquired an untouchable, museum-like character. And Spetsopoula, the small island that Niarchos bought at the end of the fifties, has been transformed into a real paradise of well-combed beaches, with bungalows, lodges, hunting grounds, a modern church, a track for karting, all grouped around the principal villa. No one has seen anything for sure on Onassis' Skorpios, except a new track of roads and the tiny old chapel which always existed on that desert island.

And why, we Athenians used to ask, is he running after Maria Callas? We had all seen them together, Onassis exuberant, courting the serious, sultry Maria, offering her a pleasant, restful, shining life of luxury, away from the always agonizing world of art and competition.

But he does not like opera, he rarely went to hear her sing, he is at heart a *bouzouki* fanatic. Was it only because she is tall and impressive-looking? Or because for other people she is the "Divina," an adored genius in the world of music, and also an undisputed personality in international society? Onassis wanted publicity, needed publicity, used publicity. Always a taker, never a giver, he used credit more than anything else, and his publicized connections with the great were the keys that opened all doors, that brought him into contact with the top bankers, the important businessmen, the millionaires, the moguls. From then on he relied on himself—on his cleverness, charm, persuasiveness—to bring off the most difficult and complicated deals.

These successes were the origin of Niarchos' obsession. He always felt that he was worth more than Onassis, that he was more solid, more serious, more important, richer. But he was not content to keep this knowledge to himself, he wanted the world to know it and Onassis to hear about it.

If only Onassis had been a different man, Niarchos might have developed into the kind of benefactor that Greece knew in the past century, generous, protective, and patriotic. He had it in him. He felt enough of a Greek to return to Greece during the war and volunteer in the Navy, a gesture which probably never even crossed Onassis' mind. At one moment, Niarchos was not only a Greek, but a good Greek. But now, that phase is over. With the coming of the Colonels, the worst traits of both the top star shipowners, and of all the discreetly following tribe, came out into the open.

Their grabbing instincts were sharpened by the Great Junta Sale. Greece was being offered at cut prices, genuine bargains to be secured in exchange for a friendly pat on uniformed backs, the Greek flag devalued below the lowest-priced Panamanian or Liberian, taxes waived, laws forgotten. It was a clever move of the isolated Colonels, an operation sure of success.

Costa and I looked again at the old photos. "What about the great friendship of Niarchos and the royal family? And of that limpet of a nephew of his, Costas Drakopoulos, the best, if not the only, friend of King Constantine?"

What about it. In a world of vacillating values and acute ambitions, past friendships, however high-level, were forgotten or put aside "for the duration." Allegiances to ideals, democracies, freedoms, and rights were dismissed as naïve and unrealistic. Greece was now what is called a "fenceless vineyard," and they all flocked to pick the fruits.

Talking about this last phenomenon, I remembered that once, some years ago, I had arrived in New York in 1964, just in time to witness the reverse, an exodus. A rumor of a new tax struck the community of Greek shipowners with such blind panic that they decided then and there to abandon New York, fly away from America, jettison offices, houses, flats. Within a few days, dozens of well-known, well-established men disappeared from the scene, taking family and children away, disposing of valuable property at any price.

"Funny lot, your countrymen . . . ," old friends whom I met in newspaper offices told me politely.

"They are not exactly my countrymen," I tried to explain, "and they are not yours either. They are special people, they are different, they do not belong to any definite nationality, and if they were not obliged to have some sort of passport, most of them would certainly choose not to have one. Their tribal instinct sends them where taxes are low, flags are cheap, credit easy, and the government in the hands of manageable people. And just as they come, so they go, scuttling away like a terror-stricken herd at the first sign of a financial change of climate. One can condemn them and dislike them and call them all sorts of names, but that does not change them or worry them in the least. It is more interesting to study them."

A whole square hatbox was labeled "Iron Curtain," and was filled with photos of Russia and Bulgaria, Hungary and Yugoslavia. The Russian ones, taken during a month's visit in 1953, were of all kinds, negatives and transparencies, black and white or color; some were my own, some taken by my companions, some offered by the Russian Press Ministry. Moscow, Leningrad, Tiflis, Sotchi; views and people and the great October

Parade; pigtailed Georgian beauties dancing, Stalin's house of birth, the Kremlin in frozen white beauty.

We had been invited, a Greek delegation, covering the full political range from a Communist writer just out of jail to me, a conservative publisher, with a sprinkling of middle-of-the-way politicians and professors and journalists, and we had been lucky in that we arrived just in time to witness the end of an era. Not that we knew it then. Stalin had died, but he was still immortal, and, godlike, he stamped every house, office, building with his presence. Portraits, photographs, busts, statues, commemorative plaques, adorned everything Russian, official and unofficial, and the queue at the Mausoleum where he lay in state beside Lenin was miles long at all hours, in any weather.

We had been allowed in, like most foreigners, from a side entrance, and had followed the slow, silent procession descending the marble staircase with its large shallow steps that plunged deeper and deeper into the crypt. Immobile soldiers held lighted torches, and the walls, lined with a precious dark gold-flecked marble, reflected the flames. As you went down in silence, the air took a new quality of freezing coldness, and there was a pharaoh-like splendor in the hidden crypt where the two crystal-clear glass cages stood side by side. Lenin, dressed in severe black, looked exactly as one would expect him to look, even to an expression of fleeting irony on his pale face, precisely finished with the small black beard. Stalin, in his plain khaki uniform, looked flabby and artificial; "not such a good resemblance," one would have said if they had been wax figures.

It had been for me an immensely interesting trip, especially as I spoke some Russian, learned thanks to a nice White Russian neighbor during the German Occupation in the momentary enthusiasm created by the epic of Stalingrad. I could read, walk around Moscow, find my way, talk to people, take photographs of them. I went to shops and markets and to the movies, and learned my way around the "Sovietskaya," a rather splendid hotel without any of the normal Western splendid hotel's comforts. It had beautiful carpets and heavy crystal chandeliers, but no porter; the central staircase had a palatial grandeur, but the lifts were erratic; and there was not one telephone directory available for the clients in the whole building. Gaudy, plushy, old-fashioned luxury was a poor substitute for the enjoyable simplicity of modern comfort, and you could not escape a stifling atmosphere of minor officialdom.

"They will never let you see the *real* Russia!" How often have I heard this, as if prisons and concentration camps were the only reality. Just by looking at people you saw enough—their houses, their shops, their faces. By talking to them. Poverty, resignation, patience were stamped on the unsmiling men and women, regimentation was as visible as if they were all in uniform, and a mild but all-pervading form of fear killed at birth any initiative and wish to tread off the beaten path even for the most innocent of purposes. There were also, alternatively, arrogance and humility. We had around us a whole group of interpreters, guides, some of them I suppose belonging to the secret police, and they all cringed before any superior and cracked the whip whenever they had the chance.

"Get up, fast!" The order had been given quite naturally in a brusque, cold voice by our guide to a middle-aged Russian sitting in the subway, and it had been obeyed quite as naturally by the man, who not only got up and fast, but walked to the farthest point of the car. And then in the other voice, the guide turned to me: "Please sit down. . . ."

He could not for his life understand why I made such a fuss over that little episode. Here we were in the fabulous Moscow

Underground, one of the wonders of the world, and I was commenting on a gesture of simple politeness. He could not understand my dismay, and I could not understand his enthusiasm. That the Moscow Underground is unique in absurd magnificence cannot be denied. But why should it be? Why the statues, the paintings, the decorative bronzes, the mosaics, the crystal chandeliers? Why should one of the stations have its wall lined with yellow onyx, illuminated from the inside, so that waiting for your train you feel that you have strayed into some kind of musical comedy finale? Why should the underground be dressed up like a palace by the same people who converted most of the real palaces into workers' playing grounds and schools?

One of the many group photographs that I fished from the lot reminded me of a visit to the "Stalin" factory and of a tall, fair-haired director, a polished western-type Russian. He had started the day mistaking me for a sound little Communist from some obscure Balkan state, rewarded for a lifetime's devotion by an invitation to visit Russia. My lame Russian was probably responsible, and he singled me out of the group and offered a special lecture during the tour of the huge factory that looked as if it produced all the machinery, the tractors, the cars, the Zim and Zis and Pobiedas that circulated in Russia. He explained, offered statistics, and finished inevitably by labeling everything as the best that is produced in any part of the world, and what is more, by the happiest, proudest workers.

I did not argue so long as we were in machinery and tractors, but when we got to the Pobiedas, uninteresting and bad copies of American cars, I said: "Well, you know, these are really not the 'best cars in the world' . . ."

He looked at me with some astonishment: "No? And where have you seen better ones, please?"

"In Detroit. . . ."

I don't think that I have ever seen a man change so immediately in expression, character, look. It was as if the time had come to throw away the mask he was wearing. He realized his mistake—maybe he had been nagged all along by a feeling that I was not behaving exactly as I should—and he smiled a broad smile, squeezed my arm, and said, before disappearing, definitely, from our party: "Oh . . . Well, my dear, I too have been to Detroit. So I leave you. Good-bye, *dorogaya*. . . ."

He had given a conspiratorial tone to his "my dear," as if he wanted to erase all the nonsense he had been telling me before.

And this is one little incident that I left out of my "Impressions from Russia," published in the *Kathimerini*, and also in English in the *Athens News* after my return.

Like every journalist, I have my own private collection of horrifying plane journeys, which I know better than to inflict upon a colleague, lest I risk being obliged to suffer in return his or her helicopter expedition in the Arctic or landing between the totems of Easter Island. But given a sympathetic audience, I come up with the one Russian word that makes me turn pale with terror. No, not KGB, or NKVD, or Siberia, but "Aeroflot." We made three trips during this journey in Russia with Soviet planes, and each one of them was, in a different way, unforgettable.

The first one was at the very beginning of our trip. We had started from Vienna, from Bad-Wieslau, an airport that looked as if it had been bombed yesterday. A black iron shed gutted by fire stood naked in the center of a field, and inside it an old Russian, a civilian employee with a long moustache, sat strug-

gling with a wooden instrument that looked like a field telephone forgotten since the First World War. There was just one
small plane waiting, perilously near a huge crater that seemed
ready to swallow it up, and nothing and nobody else around.
The horizon was empty of anything resembling a control
tower, and we waited standing in an icy wind while the Russian Consul in Vienna kept us silent company. A word from
the old man brought him to life. He made us a sign to accompany him, helped us to climb the few steps that led to the
plane, said *"Da Svidanya,"* and abandoned us. Inside the plane,
we were the only passengers. The cabin was extraordinarily
cold and bare, there was no hostess, on the seats there were
no seat belts, but on eleven of them there were cardboard
boxes, each of them containing a sandwich, a piece of cake,
and a lemon.

We were looking out to try and discover the airstrip from
which we would be taking off, when we heard the motors,
which were running smoothly, give a wild groan, then a roar,
and in a series of bumps which threw us clutching wildly at
our seats, we were off and, miraculously, up.

We sat and ate our lunch and tried to drink our lemon, as
there was nothing else, and we decided that we were going to
freeze to death. There was no hostess in whom to confide our
misery, and we were thinking of seeking out the pilot, when
he came out of his cabin and, without even giving us a good-
day or a glance, looked up at the board over the cabin door on
our side—where we saw to our extreme surprise and uneasiness
an altimeter. After that we did not dare worry him, as we believed him to be alone. At least we did not see, for the whole
trip that lasted hours, anyone else but him: that is, his quickly
turned back and his head looking at the meter.

In the mood of fatalism that grips the traveler in such cir-

Sofia, 1963. Nikita Khrushchev, guest of the Bulgarian government, with General Secretary of the Bulgarian Communist Party Zivkov and Bulgarian Prime Minister Yukov, posing for an unofficial photographer during an official party.

Mykonos, 1963. Mrs. Jacqueline Kennedy at the threshold of the writer's villa, accompanied by Prince Radziwill, one of the members of her party. Security officers and an accompanying Greek admiral are seen in the background.

Aris Onassis in a jubilant mood aboard his yacht *Christina* clowns for the benefit of social-ite Dolla Zarifi, and for the photographer.

Stavros Niarchos, thoughtful, casual, and bourgeois, stands beside his niece Helen Dra-kopoulos, with the pine-cov-ered slopes of Spetsopoula as a background.

cumstances, we promised each other that if we did arrive in Moscow, we would take a vow never to "Aeroflot" again.

Human nature being what it is, two weeks later we were flying from Moscow to Tiflis. This time it was much worse. For seven interminable hours we traveled in a plane that was burning with heat and from all signs was going to burst into flames at any second. A smell of petrol filled the cabin, and very soon it was quite difficult to breathe and quite impossible to touch anything metallic without being scorched. This time we never saw the pilot, who we guessed must be trying without success to extinguish the fire. We were going to explode any moment, and it would serve us right for not keeping our promise. We sat silent, accepting this premature hell, not even daring to murmur "never again Aeroflot."

It was a good thing that we did not, because we were subjected to one more "Aeroflot" treatment, this time from Leningrad to Helsinki. The trip was short, but quite as unforgettable as the others. It was January, and the visibility was so bad as to be virtually nonexistent. The pilot decided to fly right down among the tops of dark spiky trees, very nearly grazing them, to be sure he was on the right way and nearer land than space. As clumps of taller trees loomed suddenly, forming dark impassable walls, he just jumped over them in bloodcurdling leaps, missing them by inches.

I never returned to Russia, not because of "Aeroflot" or because I did not want to, but because my traveling was dictated by events more than by personal choice. I got in and out of the Iron Curtain countries for short visits, and in May 1962 I spent a few quite interesting days in Bulgaria, at the time Khrushchev was there on an official tour. During this visit I had a characteristic experience with Iron Curtain bureaucracy.

The very first day I arrived I said I needed a photographer. They asked me what for, and I explained that I wanted photographs of today's and tomorrow's State receptions to send back to the two papers.

"We will provide you in time with all the necessary photographs," they promised politely, and they went on explaining that it was quite impossible, even unthinkable, for me to have my own photographer taking pictures during the reception, and that anyhow, any photographs taken would have to be screened and authorized before being given to the press for publication.

I said "all right" and forgot all about it, but that evening, just for fun, I slipped a Leica into my evening bag. And later, standing in a circle around the group of Russian officials which had arrived and was being shot at from every angle by a battery of cameras, I joined in and rather diffidently took a few pictures. Then a few more. I smiled at Khrushchev, and he smiled back. Then I turned to Yukov, the Bulgarian Prime Minister, and Zivkov, then General Secretary of the Bulgarian Communist Party; then to a group of solemn, solid, satin-encased Russian and Bulgarian ladies. I stopped because I had no more film, and an informal press conference was taking place. Again my poor Russian gave me rich dividends, and I got Khrushchev practically to myself. He was one of the very few completely relaxed Russians that I had ever met. He smiled, talked, joked, drank and called for drinks and offered them, and rambled on while officials followed him, silent and stony-faced, and interpreters and journalists, mostly foreign correspondents, sauntered around. That day he was in an especially mischievous mood, and when I introduced myself as a Greek, he proceeded to recite in Russian a long and tedious version of one of Aesop's fables. And then he asked me to give his best wishes to all his Greek friends now in jail because they were good Communists, and to tell them that they would soon be out.

"You Greeks are wonderful people . . . but imperialists! No, not important ones. We have important imperialist countries with big stomachs, and we have small imperialist countries with small stomachs. You are a small country with a small stomach. . . ."

The next morning I went to the special Press Bureau and asked innocently for photographs of the previous evening. They were not yet ready, I was told, but I should not worry, I would get them tomorrow, or the day after.

I did not worry but I went and bought film and started a photographic orgy. In and out of doors, during banquets and receptions, on formal occasions and at informal parties, I never stopped. It was impossible that nobody saw me, but I suppose that the ones who did could never imagine that I was not fully accredited with all the necessary papers and permissions. They did not even think of asking any questions, seeing the smiles ping-pong between me and Ministers and Prime Ministers, and the Secret Police allowed me to get right under Khruschchev's nose—who, during the entire visit, continued playing the role of a heavily humorous "little father" type, burly, pleasant, and reassuring for anyone who met him for the first time. But it was not my first time, and on this Dr. Jekyll performance I could superimpose the snarling Mr. Hyde in the Palais de Chaillot in Paris two years before, when red-faced and screaming in hatred and indignation, he tore the Summit Conference apart.

The visit nearly over, on the last day I made quite a fuss in the Press Bureau: I had not yet received a single one of the photographs promised. They were very sorry, they did not understand the reason for the delay, but they would mail them to Athens the moment they got them, I was not to worry. I did not worry in the least, and the articles I wrote for the *Messimvrini* were accompanied by masses of photographs.

They had come out very well, and I sent a number of them back to the Bulgarian Press Bureau. I never received any myself, but by then maybe they had realized that I did not need them.

Every trip behind the Iron Curtain awoke in me basically the same sentiment. Pity. Pity for the people who lived there and were subjected from the day of their birth to a continuous, sly, brain-washing therapy that left most of them like well-treated patients in a modern psychiatric hospital, walking around life with a resigned half-smile, in a tractable mood that led them to accept whatever was offered—work, entertainment, punishment, rewards—with the same resigned apathy.

I had seen the same signs on the faces of the people in Lisbon's drab streets: the same dismal shops, the same enveloping atmosphere of dusty order and silent boredom in every hotel, in Belgrade or Kiev or Sofia.

My revulsion at any form of totalitarian government was so deep that it was the one subject I could not discuss in cold blood. That it could be accepted as beneficial in any form, under any circumstance, seemed to me the height of hypocrisy or ignorance. That democracy was a system fraught with dangers, no one could question, but so was life. And only a deep death wish, a premature craving for the peace and quiet of the tomb, could explain the comfort some people derived from living in caged silence.

All that sounded superfluous and self-evident before the coup of April 21. Poor innocents, we thought we were still members of an alliance that had taken up arms to fight dictatorships and totalitarianism, and was still keeping a military force called NATO with that purpose in mind.

If anyone had asked us why we fought in the last war, we would probably have made it clear that we fought against the kinds of regimes that send people to concentration camps, take control of civilian life, inflict martial law and press censorship, enjoy degrading the individual, putting him under the supervision of secret police and spies, arresting him without charges, searching his home without warrant. By no flight of the imagination could we have conceived that twenty years later, after we finished fighting the Fascists, the Nazis, and the Communists, we would become the victim of the first postwar dictatorship, armed and recognized by the Western powers. What we had to accept now was the kind of "law and order" that Mussolini had offered us. The same kind of advice, given—and taken—thirty years ago, would at least have saved Greece from years of suffering and destruction.

To be frank, it took us some time to realize that we had been well and properly sold out by our former allies, and we believed—at least Costa and I did—during the first days and weeks of the coup that America, the greatest "democratic" power in the world, would come to the rescue of the unarmed majority of the Greeks, or at least would refrain from helping and supporting the Colonels.

A long, intimate, love-hate relationship with America had developed for me during the years of constant coming and going, of meeting Americans in Greece and meeting them again in America, of reading about America, hearing, learning, seeing the new country becoming ever richer, more powerful, and step by step, year by year, taking over and becoming the sovereign power of the Western world.

As a traveler, I loved the country. When I first saw New York, arriving by ship in 1939, I fell into a wide-eyed enchantment out of which I have never recovered. "New York is not America," the statement which pursues you throughout the United States, is most inaccurate. The truth is that only New

York is America. You can imagine all the other cities, full of memories and imitations of the old world; you recognize France in New Orleans, the Orient in San Francisco, and England everywhere else, and in Washington you get big chunks of Athens and Rome; but in New York, in Manhattan, in the magical tower city, you are confronted by a new form of breathtaking beauty that nothing can make you visualize in advance. No photos, films, descriptions, can do justice to the sight of the forest of towers and skyscrapers rising in grace and majesty, shafts of glass and metal gold-studded with window panes reflecting the rays of an invisible sun. "Yes, but I would not like to live there," is another of the statements that belittle New York's beauty, as much as it would that of the Taj Mahal. Few people would want to live there, either.

Memories of places and people merge in the postwar years. It was usually New York and Washington, and the United Nations, and the familiar newspaper offices, and the Greek Embassy on Massachusetts Avenue, with changing ambassadors and similar problems, with the Press Conference in the White House and President Truman sitting in the same impressive room where President Roosevelt had sat, with cocktail parties and press luncheons, and hours and days and sometimes weeks waiting in the sterilized corridors of the UN for a decision of the Assembly, usually on the Cyprus question.

I did manage short trips to California and the South, and at one time, in 1957, I got away from the usual haunts for two whole weeks to take part in a summer seminar in deserted but quite lovely Princeton. The subject was "NATO and the Mediterranean Problem," and we had been invited, fifty participants, between the ages of thirty and fifty, not connected with any official position, so that nothing could prevent us from talking "quite freely." The whole conference was to be kept severely off the record, without any press or radio coverage, and even the journalists taking part were asked not to report on the proceedings. The idea was to create an intimate climate of confidence that would give birth to provocative discussions, even if possible to constructive quarrels.

One rather unusual detail was that our group consisted of forty-nine men and me. This solitary feminine presence was soon accepted and passed unnoticed, and only on the first day provoked a slightly embarrassing incident. One of the many professors who were acting as hosts was briefing us about the entertainments and sports that would be available to the members of the seminar between conferences and talks.

"There is also the swimming pool, open all day. . . ." Suddenly he stopped and looked at me:

"As I was saying, there is the swimming pool. Hm . . . You are of course welcome to go there. But I must warn you that here in Princeton, you are not allowed to wear, hm, a swimming suit. You are expected to swim in the nude, like everybody else. . . ."

I looked up and reassured him with a smile that I had got the message. There was to be no swimming for me.

That seminar proved impossibly dull. The absence of press and TV, and the fact that nobody bothered with it, instead of helping us to concentrate, made us feel that we were wasting our time. The only consolation was the quality of many of the participants, eminent professors and journalists, and the presence of J. Robert Oppenheimer. He was an immediately impressive man. There was no taking him for one moment for anything else but a genius, and talking with him you felt the impact of a rapier-like intelligence blended with profound human charm. He had also many reasons to be disturbed and unhappy, not so much because he himself was considered to be a "controversial" person, but because of the reasons that made America distrust him.

Once I came very near to becoming the publisher of the Greek edition of the *Reader's Digest*. It had been brewing a long time, I had been in Pleasantville, New York, and from Pleasantville editors kept coming to Athens. We made arrangements and discussed details, and I was getting a wealth of information and technical advice. I was quite interested, especially as it could prove to be a very lucrative affair, but had some misgivings about the "How happy I was the day I broke my leg" type of article. But I had the necessary machinery to print it and all the translators, and as the copy and art work were provided, it would be quite an easy job. At least it seemed so. We were going through the last details with two important editors and we were ready to clinch the agreement and decide on the date of publication, when somewhere at that stage I must have failed. There was a "test" atmosphere which I sensed, and the questions had taken a sentimental tone.

"How much will you love the *Reader's Digest*?"

"Love? Why should I love it?"

"But you do love the *Kathimerini*, don't you?"

"Well, yes, I suppose I do, but that's different."

I was never quite sure of what exactly happened after that, except that the date of publication was postponed twice, and then the whole matter was quietly shelved. The *Reader's Digest* never appeared in Greek, edited by me or by anyone else. But I remained with the suspicion that what had broken the agreement was my telling an unforgivable truth.

It was the kind of truth most Americans find very difficult to accept, even to understand; especially those who are becoming increasingly, disturbingly more American. That natural environment plays a major role in the development of mind and body cannot be disputed—the extreme example is the fact that no human being of high intelligence has ever been able to create any work of genius in the enveloping lethargy of intense heat on the Equator, or in the freezing numbing world of the Arctic. If you pinpointed on a map the birthplaces of the great men of the human race, you would find them in a clearly defined belt in most continents, with Europe the unchallenged provider of geniuses, the most densely populated with philosophers, writers, poets, mathematicians, sculptors, painters, musicians, scientists, and genuine democrats.

Whatever the errors and the weaknesses of the old continent, it was still there that democracy was born and reared. We Greeks started it about twenty-five centuries ago, and the idea spread but never went far beyond the European continent. We Europeans invented the concept of democracy, taught democracy, fought for democracy, and, not without ups and downs, halts and stops, at times really practiced democracy. It never infected Asia and was never satisfactorily transplanted either to South Africa or South America. And now, one can be excused for having doubts about how it is faring in North America. The whole atmosphere of the great country is changing, and so are many of her children. Already the chemistry of the land, the air, the water, the earth, the food is producing a new kind of easily recognizable human beings. There is some justice in the fact that many of the salient features of the native who was thought exterminated are imperceptibly creeping back, and that very often you see an old American, tall, skinny, with a deeply furrowed face and searching eyes, who could easily wear a red Indian chief's feathers. A new breed of humans is coming to be good-looking and strong, well coordinated, swift on their feet, clever on a horse. But is the subtle change influencing only the American's external appearance? What about his love of colorful festivities, parades, and dressing-ups, his willingness to believe magicians and astrologers and preachers of fancy religions? What of his weakness for guns and pistols? Is he reverting through the molding of all-pervading natural influences to primitive instincts, with uncontrollable fits of hate or panic that might at a moment's notice change a placid family man into a creature of blind violence and cruelty?

How safe is our Western world in his hands? Europe has been the leader for centuries and, from Athens or Rome, Constantinople or Venice, Spain, France, or England, has influenced the destiny of the civilized world—not always for the happiness of its long-suffering inhabitants, drawn into the wars and fights of continuously feuding emperors and kings. But still, Europe has led the world toward a better life, and it has never before relinquished the responsibility of this all-important leadership. Never before, until now, when the inheritor suddenly looms terrifyingly powerful, and just as terrifyingly confused. Not that America has not spectacular successes to show in space travel and science and industry and the arts, where it is leading the way and opening new paths. But again these are the departments where first-generation Europeans still work and help and offer their brains and experience. Where the new Americans are mostly on their own, in politics and in diplomacy and in the State Department and the maze of the Pentagon and the hideouts of the CIA, the results are less reassuring. More problems have been created than solved during these last postwar years, either through capricious and irresponsible intervention, or through hypocritical and just as irresponsible nonintervention.

That the mistakes are genuine, the bungling involuntary, is the one redeeming aspect of the situation. It is not aggressiveness, or vicious imperialism, as suspicious Moscow would have it, but just lack of experience and tradition enmeshed in a plodding bureaucracy.

All this one must not say to the Americans, even to those who feel it and know it and understand it and realize the significance of the Bay of Pigs, and the Vietnams, and Greece. They deplore everything, but they do not want to hear about it.

Between the end of October and the middle of November we were left quite alone, and small incidents like the coincidence of a near-visit and a non-visit by two Greek-Americans took on a disproportionate importance. The first, who managed to charm the guard into allowing her to talk to me from the landing without stepping into the house, was Deppy Messinezi, one of my oldest friends. She was as slim and chic as ever, looking every inch the travel editor for *Vogue* she now was, based in New York but running around the world, lively as a whippet.

As usual, when the circumstances are too unusual (the dialogue between astronauts is an example of the banality that results in too extraordinary a situation), we just exchanged familiar phrases, but we enjoyed our little talk, and I was delighted to receive the first present for many a day, a Mary Quant lipstick.

Deppy, an Epirote by birth, was now a Greek-American of quality. Clever, hard-working, courageous, and infectiously gay, with enormous shining black eyes and a short-clipped curly head of hair, she had had a difficult life after a disastrous marriage that left her a young divorcee in loneliness and poverty. Her success in fashion and journalism was the result of untiring effort and exquisite good taste. Starting as more or less an amateur "shop-hound," she graduated into a full-fledged professional editor. Thanks to her, though she would never admit it, I had seen myself in *Vogue,* in an issue of October 1954, which carried a feature called "Famous Greeks." The complimentary caption, under the more than flattering photograph, was certainly Deppy's work.

The non-visit of Mr. Tom Pappas was a very different matter. One morning the maid arrived quite excited: we were going to have a visitor! An important one, the guard had told her; "*The* Mr. Tom Pappas."

She was quite crestfallen when she was told to go and say that we didn't want to see Mr. Pappas, that we had been asking to see the children, and our lawyer, and friends, and no one had been allowed to come, so we did not see any reason to accept the visit of Mr. Tom Pappas.

But the guard insisted. The visit had been arranged through the "authorities," and he had no means of stopping it. My husband went to the door and explained that if the guard could not stop Mr. Pappas we would, and that telling him to go away via the maid would probably hurt Mr. Pappas' feelings more than whatever the authorities would find to tell him as an excuse to cancel the visit.

Anyhow, he never came, and we were not sorry. He was a Greek-American, a clever, cheerful, back-slapping fellow with contacts in high political circles, who appeared on the Greek scene full of plans and ideas, to disappear suddenly for indefinite periods of time, and who was now a warm supporter of the Junta. What he wanted to come and see us for we did not know, and we never learned. Not that we could not guess. Many visitors had come to the office during the first months of the coup (Spiro Skouras, a life-long friend of Tom Pappas, among them) to offer sympathy and some kind of help, which was always linked with the advice that we should be more "logical." They could not understand that we were not in a mood to be logical. And these people, more often than not, asked a question which always sounded to me like the height of absurdity.

"But Helen . . . how long can you go on *not* publishing?" How long? In the world of publishers, it is the contrary that can present a problem. How long, in difficult circumstances, can one *go on* publishing? But where lies the difficulty of "not-publishing"?

What they meant was that at a certain point we should recover from the suicidal mania that drove us to ruin. They still had their logic on, while we felt at war, wearing invisible uniforms. We felt that Greece as we knew it had collapsed on April 21, and that in a different, less exciting, but quite as dangerous a way, we were again taken over by enemies.

On their side, they believed, or wanted to believe, that it was only an episode, that life was going on, and that it was quite unthinkable to sacrifice a splendidly lucrative business for the sake of a few stupid officers, who would be off the scene any time, and who anyway were not really as bad as all that.

And there we stopped the discussion and parted roads. In our minds they were as bad as all that, and worse. They were driving Greece into a new era of bitterness and hate, without the justification—how ironic it sounds—of war.

We spoke a lot about the war, Costa and I, during our long evenings together. We could have been on different planets during the years 1941-1944, so different had been our lives and our experiences.

Costa had been in submarines, mostly patrolling in the Aegean, carrying troops and commandos, arms and money for the underground, meeting guerrillas in deserted coves, and all the time chasing and being chased. Moonlight, the lovely, silver, shining, romantic pride of our seas, spelt danger. Surfacing at night, he had to hide in the night shadows of some deserted island coast, and he described the dark velvety nights when, standing in silent vigil on the deck, he scanned the horizon for a subtle change in the quality of darkness that could mean an enemy ship. Of his sinking an Italian destroyer in Samos harbor he talked very little, though it was an acknowledged feat of daring and luck. The port was full of enemy ships when he slunk through a mined passage.

I had nothing of the kind to tell. I had done very little underground work; my work in the hospital, and then at a Red Cross Children's Center, had kept me very busy.

Like everybody else in Athens, I had lived through the nightmare of the first winter of the Occupation. It was difficult to believe that thousands could drift peacefully from hunger to starvation and from starvation to death without realizing it, without fighting, stealing, killing for food. During the first months, the Germans took away everything, not only to feed the Occupation Army, but also to send to the German troops in Africa. Soon there was no meat, no fish, no eggs, no milk, no oil, no potatoes, no bread. The daily rations became smaller and less nourishing, people relied on vegetables and roots and weak soups made from gruel. The good weather, and the natural frugality of the Greeks, helped the summer to pass without many victims, but when winter came the lack of protein made itself felt. For many it was too late. Thousands died, without protesting, in silent agony, dazed and numb, without any wish or strength to fight for life. One saw them in the streets, stopping in frozen immobility, and then just falling down and dying in the quietest possible manner. And usually you could do nothing about it, as there was no transport available of any kind, except the closed van that collected the corpses and took them to the cemetery. I saw with my own eyes, in the middle of Patissia Road, a young mother curl up on the pavement and die with a tiny living baby held tight in her arms. An old woman took it away, grimly confident that it would present no problem, as it was whimpering weakly and looking at the world with enormous, glazed, already unseeing eyes.

Once a very young man fainted on the pavement, in front of the flat I was living in at that time. Some passers-by helped me to bring him in, and while he was lying down I fed him some hot broth with a spoon. After a while, he opened his eyes and started crying. Not with despair, but with happiness, with youth, with the feeling of life ebbing back. One small cup of broth was what separated him from death, and he came to see me after a few days, alive and well.

Next spring, that phase of the war was over. The people knew now what they had to expect if they resigned themselves to roots and crumbs. Some started to sell all their belongings for food, others left Athens and went to live in the country, where they planted every inch of earth and garden; a thriving black market was organized with the Italians, and the basic problem of survival was solved.

With a memory that is often a capricious chooser, I cannot try to evoke the years of the German Occupation without the picture of my eleven-year-old "con" genius cropping up at some stage. I spent years of harassing work in the Red Cross Center in Pangrati, but only that morning has remained unforgettable, vivid and sharp in all its details.

It was in 1943. We were already in the second year of Occupation, and I was in charge of a "Distribution Center" of the Red Cross which fed about a thousand children daily in three groups: newly born through 3 months' infants, then 3-12 months' infants, then from the one-year-olds up to the twelve-year-olds. There was very little to do in the hospitals, and most of the Red Cross nurses had taken over this kind of work, as the uniform helped them to circulate freely and keep some authority in the agonizing duty of choosing which children were really poor and starved and had a right to the rations of milk and semolina and gruel, and which had to be sent away, because they were only hungry and their parents could provide enough food to keep them alive.

In this chaotic atmosphere of endless queues, crying babies, sullen mothers, and fighting children, a little angel of an eleven-year-old boy arrived one morning, all joy and excitement: "Sister, Sister, an old lady is going to give us cakes!"

Haltingly he explained that the old lady who lived at the big house at the corner of the street had sent him over to tell me that as today was the birthday of her granddaughter she had made some cakes, and she saved quite a few to give to the poor children of the Canteen. Would one of the ladies come and take the cakes? He would show the way.

These glad tidings spread like wildfire, and enthusiasm, mingled with the agony of who was going to get a cake and who was not, stopped all the proceedings. Considering the importance of the mission, I decided to go myself and at once. The boy leading merrily in front, we arrived at our destination in less than five minutes. The house, with a little garden and a smart front door, showed a certain air of prosperity. "She lives on the second floor," he said, and left me. I rang the bell, and when the door opened after a certain lapse of time, I heard a not very encouraging voice ask who I was, and what did I want. "I am the nurse from the Red Cross Center," I answered, and I was told rather grudgingly to come up. A few moments later the vision of cakes and goodies had vanished into thin air. The woman had no granddaughter, she had no sugar or flour to spare, she had baked no cakes and could not for the life of her understand the reason for this stupid joke. Neither could I, so after a few minutes of desultory conversation interspersed with apologies, I begged pardon for troubling her and went back, puzzling all the way over what seemed a pointless and cruel joke. To my surprise at the Center I found the excitement at fever pitch. "Where are the cakes? Who is bringing them? Do they look good . . . ?"

I shook my head and started explaining, when a voice in sudden understanding cried out: "The wretch! . . . Quick, run after him . . . He stole the baking pan!"

What had happened during the time I was conferring with the old lady was that he had gone running back to the Center, always the obliging little boy, and had said that I had sent him to take a big baking pan to put the cakes in because there were so many. And under the benevolent eyes of everyone present, he had selected the biggest possible pan in the canteen kitchen, a giant of gleaming copper. And had vanished with it. To sell it, to offer it to his family, to show it off to the gang, who knows? His plan had been a marvel of simplicity, every detail had been thought of and timed, and at no moment did he risk discovery. No one would have trusted a pan or a dish to him if he had just asked for one "to fill it with cakes," so he had devised a foolproof scheme, and had executed it with masterly perfection.

I have often wondered what became of him, and how his early talent developed.

In mid-November, Costa was again allowed to go out. The guard one morning told the maid to tell the Kyrios Loundras that "he was free."

It was a great relief for me, and it changed my whole schedule. I now had direct contact with the world, and twice a day on Costa's return for lunch and dinner we exchanged our crop of news. One of the best contributions he brought back, the very first day, was that our standpoint had been recognized on the international juridical level and published in a report of the International Commission of Jurists dated October 28, 1967. It was quite long, but one paragraph was enough for me:

> Mrs. Vlachos is clearly not responsible for the fact that there has been a military take-over and that as direct consequence her newspapers were arbitrarily deprived overnight of their *raison d'être* and prevented from discharging their responsibility. In the circumstances she could not do otherwise than suspend publication.

The satisfaction was moral, and we cherished it even if we knew that it would not influence the Greek courts or save us a single penny.

On coming home from the outside world, Costa usually did not have much political news to tell—I was the better informed through listening to the foreign stations—but he was again in touch with the children, the family, the office, and he took over where we had left it the task of finding the necessary money to pay for our expenses, our liabilities, our newly acquired debts. Being secluded in a small house worried me much less than it did my husband, both morally and physically. The greatest part of my adult life had been spent sitting behind a desk, reading, writing, talking to people, telephoning. And part of it I was doing right now, reading and writing at leisure, hearing the radio, talking with Costa. I was always an instinctive cave-dweller. I needed very little exercise to keep fit, I rarely if ever went for a walk, and if I did it was in cities to look at houses, streets, shops. A good sailor and swimmer, I loved the sea, but there again I was attracted by the bare rocks and the naked islands, and I had started to haunt the barest and rockiest of them all, Mykonos, more than thirty years ago, before anyone had even heard of the name.

Also I had the company of my two dogs and a young cat. As a child at home, I grew up with Alsatians, then when I married I had a couple of Airedales, one of which, Ricky, was during the war years the only collaborator in the family. Poor thing, he could not understand why I did not give him enough to eat during the dreadful first winter of the German Occupation, and he grew thin and desperate. I was quite relieved to see him make friends with a German officer who stayed in a house nearby.

Cocker spaniels and a collection of nondescripts of all colors and sizes came after the war, and then I fell for a dachshund puppy, and remained faithful to that enchanting breed ever after. The first day I came to the office with the blonde shining little sausage, an old employee, also a dog lover, looked at it with distaste: "I suppose that is the kind of dog you have to keep in these modern low-ceilinged houses. . . ."

More than dogs, cats were a "must" in our family. There was never a question of choosing between the two, and we never found any difficulty in keeping both dogs and cats at the same time, and never thought of starting a cat-lover versus a dog-lover discussion.

The dogs were ours. We felt secure in their affection, their loyalty and enthusiasm; we enjoyed their tireless flattery, and the pleasant feeling that you had them near you whenever you wanted them, whenever you called them, lovely to play with, to touch and to hug. And as they started in life as that most delightful of nature's productions, a darling of an irresistible bundle of messy and destructive charm, we were constantly bringing back home one puppy or another, knowing all the time that it would develop into a friend, a burden, and a problem.

The cats owned us. We tried very hard to win their friendship and confidence, were extremely proud when we achieved it, and never took many liberties, even with the scruffiest and ugliest of the breed. Brave, resourceful, elegant, clever, they decided how to treat us, and they wavered from icy and bored indifference to sudden clinging and oversentimental affection. We all treasured the company of an intelligent cat, and it was a rare thing to find my father, in his office or writing an article, without the presence on his desk or somewhere quite near of a cat sitting in immobility, offering the satisfying accompaniment of a furry purr.

From a succession of innumerable cats of all breeds and colors, one, the big brown tabby Persian Vanya, left the most durable memory. When he died, his obituary was published with all honors in the *Kathimerini*:

Vanya died two days ago, like a human, from a heart attack. He was not old, had just turned eight, but he had lived a life of excesses, quarrels, love affairs, battles, disappearances: "LOST: Large male brown tabby Persian cat." How often this announcement has been published in Athenian newspapers since he was brought over from France in the summer of 1947. He was then a small furry ball that had been mewing desperately from Marseilles to Piraeus in passionate protest at the sudden lack of a mother, at the new solitude, at milk in a saucer.

"I have not slept for three nights," George Vlachos announced proudly on his arrival. There was nothing he would not endure for the sake of a cat.

In his documents, the little Parisian was registered as Vanille de Charade. But a male cat could not possibly go about the Athenian roofs answering to the name of Vanille, and the change to Vanya was effected on the spot. And Vanya started growing, and could not stop growing. He became a huge brown tiger, with an immense head, minute ears, a flat rusty red nose, golden eyes, magnificent silken fur, and an excellent, well-balanced, kindly disposition. That first year, we misunderstood him. He was enormous, but

inexperienced and innocent, and he fell in love with a tor-
toiseshell of a tramp who led him on, disdained his passion,
and spat at him in catty scorn. "That Parisian is going to
cover us with ridicule," was the reaction of the family, while
Vanya sat back and suffered both cats and men to gossip
about him. And then came that second triumphant winter.
Vanya, crouched on his soft cushion, suddenly realized that
his time, his night had come. He left warmth, protection,
and caresses behind him and started out silently for the big
adventure. One day, two days, five, ten days. "Vanya has
got lost. . . ."

But Vanya, thin, scratched, with his coat lusterless with
dirt, returned one dawn, proud and silent. Lost in his
thoughts, he ate, slept, and vanished again. And in a few
months' time, his worth started showing. In all the court-
yards around, kittens appeared with our Vanya's brown
color, bushy tails, square little faces. Vanya had imposed
himself. And he advanced into life knowing exactly what
he wanted out of it. Food, sleep and caresses, battles and love.

Once, after a month's disappearance that brought him back
in a peculiarly fearful condition, we thought of locking him
up. But an English book on *Cat Breeding and General Man-
agement*, which we studied carefully, stopped us: "In order
to keep a Persian male cat in good health, you must provide
him during the year with at least twenty females. . . ."

Twenty females? We opened the door and let him out
into the night. "Go, Vanya, and meet your fate . . . !" But
he won and survived. Though he was the gentlest animal,
he was dangerous and savage when quarreling, and his last
enemy, a mustard yellow gangster, turned tail and left after
a duel that disturbed the whole street for weeks and left
Vanya with multiple wounds, difficulty in walking, and ears
like Venetian lace. After that, the whole area was his, and
no other male cat ever dared to come near.

And Vanya did not go after adventures any more, he

waited for them to come. Even this last year when he started showing signs of weariness, he was always available, always willing. Just lately, two very young females, a blotchy grey and white and a lustrous black, arrived on the terrace to look for him. It was as if they had heard the older cats say: "Let us face facts! . . . The old Vanya has never been equaled by any of the new generation . . . !" And they had come to seek him. Their mothers were right. Not one of the male cats that lived in the Vlachos home, and there must have been a whole regiment, ever equaled him in flashing, sudden, violent, and effective erotic skill.

The two little ones, however, were his last adventure. He fell ill. He stopped eating and sat very quietly in a corner with his head bent low and half-closed eyes. Poor Vanya, we plagued him with all the drugs and tyrannies we employ for humans in similar cases, but to no avail.

The most beautiful cat in Athens—we can say it now that he is dead—the kindest and the most positive in his ambitions, has started on his last journey. The young male cats of the neighborhood perhaps do not know that the area is theirs again. The Parisian who had conquered the female cat population of Athens has lost his first and last battle.

And thanks to Vanya, I had the occasion of a Walter Mitty type of victory. He had just come back in a disgraceful state from one of his epic love battles, had been seen by the vet, had been ignominiously shaved all around the ears and given a shot of penicillin, with another coming later on. This I was to give. I had long been demoted from a surgeon's head nurse to a veterinary's occasional aid.

Late in the evening, the vet called me, asking for news of Vanya.

"I gave him three shots," I told him, "and each time double the quantity you told me to."

"Have you gone mad?"

"No, not quite. An Englishman told me to. He came home for lunch, had a look at Vanya, and said that you had been stingy with the penicillin."

"Really? And may I ask who gave you this extraordinary bit of advice?"

There was my cue. I offered it with as modest a voice as I could manage: "Sir Alexander Fleming."

It was exactly true. That day I had given a small lunch party in his honor, and, contrary to his usual rather silent and retiring self, he was in especially high spirits. We did not know it then, but he was heading toward marriage with charming Amalia Voureka, a Greek scientist who had been his assistant, and she was also there. It was a beautiful sparkling Athenian October day, and he enjoyed everything, even the sight of a sick cat.

In Athens I always missed a zoo. There must be few capitals or even cities as big and important as Athens without one. For a short time during the First World War, a small zoo was started near the Phaleron Delta, just opposite to where the race course is situated now, but it closed for lack of food and water during the blockade of 1916.

I remember it, or think I do, because the family never tired of repeating my first stinging comment uttered at the age of three. I had been taken to the zoo by the one and only ugly aunt provided by both my mother's and father's families. I don't think she would have been considered ugly today, because she was thin and elegant, with a bony but quite striking face. But at that time, when beauty meant cupid mouths, round eyes, and curls, she was the pitied exception.

That day, as the fashion dictated, she was wearing a large hat and was swathed in a veil. I had been going around the cages enthralled, but kept coming back to the monkeys and looking at them and then at my aunt. At the end I asked, in unquestionable innocence:

"Why don't the monkeys wear veils, too?"

Nothing more to wait for

ATHENS: *December, 1967*

By the end of November, we were certain that my trial would
never take place. Twice it had been announced to the foreign
correspondents during the weekly press conferences, and we
would hear from the BBC that "The trial of Mrs. Helen Vlachos, the publisher charged with insulting the authorities, has
been fixed for October 24," and then "for November 12," and
we would wait from day to day for some more definite sign to
materialize, but the dates passed and nothing happened.

The general impression in Athens was that Andreas Papandreou, Mikis Theodorakis, and Helen Vlachos would never be
brought to court, primarily because of the interest they would
create in the foreign press, also for fear of embarrassing disclo-
sures and, in my case, for fear of ridicule. A solemn panel of
militarily garbed judges, discussing the word "clown" as an in-
sult to Brigadier Minister Pattakos (present and looking the
clown he was), was difficult to envisage.

It was no use waiting for the trial. I would either remain
indefinitely under house arrest or be liberated on the condition
of remaining silent.

"You have to get out of Greece. . . ."

It was my mother and my husband who started me on my
journey. While I tried to persuade them that I had made up

my mind to sit back, and write, and read and bask away into more or less contented idleness, they would not begin to believe me. Maybe because I had been so very busy all my life, my inactivity was automatically labeled as an intolerable misery which would finish by breaking my spirit.

I sent messages to my mother that I was quite all right and reasonably happy and enjoyed certain aspects of my "harem" life, but she did not believe me. And I said and repeated approximately the same things to my husband, and he did not believe me either. I had to be miserable and bored and unhappy, but I was hiding it so as not to add to their own worries. They knew that I was accustomed to meet people, to write, to work, to be free, and they believed that any action would be denied to me in Greece so long as the Colonels were in power.

I had to get away. The most thrilling aspect of this decision was that it was taken by the most conservative of men, by Costa, who with undue haste had drifted into middle age, silently condemning any kind of youthful flutter, choosing severe clothes, discouraging any tendency towards eccentricity, avoiding noisy parties, disliking on me anything conspicuous, insisting on my keeping my hair white.

And now there he was, talking of escape and of hideouts, avoiding the police, slinking out at night, not only accepting that I should try such an adventure, but discussing it with the seriousness of an officer planning the escape of a fellow officer. There was no question of both of us leaving. One had to stay behind and take care of the children, the family, the houses, the newspaper installations. Our fortune was dwindling, but there was still quite a lot of it, and it was important to make it last as long as possible. No, I was the one to get out; I had friends and connections in the outside world, I spoke foreign languages, I was familiar with the journalists and publishers of the free world. Costa quipped about it.

"In the last war, you stayed in Greece and I went and fought and came back and liberated you. Now you go out and do the same."

We are both very undramatic people, and we did our best not to let our feelings get out of hand, treating most of the preparations as a joke in which we did not really believe. But we went on planning all the same. It was not getting out of the house that worried me, because there were several ways to get through the guards. It was getting out of the country. I knew that many friends believed that once out of the house I could ask asylum in one of the foreign Embassies and with their aid get out of the country, but I doubted it very much, and I was later to be proved right.

Former friends, proprietors of yachts, helicopters, and private planes, had kept safely away from our misguided path, taking great care not to ask for news of us or to convey any sympathy. So we knew where we stood with them. The only solution I could see was to get papers in some other name and brazen it out. In Greece I was much better known as a name than as a face. Television had not yet entered into our lives, my picture was never published in our newspapers, and very rarely in the others, so I was confident that with some change in my appearance I could pass unrecognized.

The trouble was that I could not make up my mind. It was the hardest decision that I had ever had to make in my life. It was not a question of fear, as there was very little danger involved, and if at any stage of my escape I got caught, I would only be back where I started, in Greece, under house arrest or in prison. It was not the failure of the venture that frightened me, it was its success: a success that would separate me for who knows how long from my husband, my family, my home, my friends, Athens, Greece, from everything that was my life. I thought of books, possessions, souvenirs of a lifetime, of rooms which bore the evidence of the passing years, even of old clothes linked with memories, familiar and friendly, which would all have to be left behind. It was not the beginning of a new life, it was the end of a very nice one.

I doubt very much that I would finally have taken the decision, if there had not been the disastrous failure of King Constantine's countercoup.

During those first days of December, whispers of some imminent change were gliding all over Athens, and every evening Costa brought back a harvest of unconfirmed but wildly optimistic rumors. The generals . . . the King . . . the Americans . . . someone was going to do something, any day now. The maid brought her own contribution from the Kolonaki market. The butcher, who had friends in the Army, had heard a strange story and was confiding it to a circle of select clients. It had happened during a banquet given by top members of the Junta at a military unit out of Athens. King Constantine was the guest of honor. Things were going smoothly when one of the officers, who was sitting near the King, noticed that his wine glass was empty. He looked around for a bottle, and failing to see one, he made a gesture to a waiter who was standing at the other end of the room . . . and at that precise moment three Junta ministers jumped up, drawing their pistols. They had mistaken the gesture for a signal.

A signal for what? we wondered. But still we waited, postponing the taking of any decision until the ill-fated December 13 came, and we knew that there was no reason to wait for anything any more.

That day everything was calm and quiet until about ten o'clock in the morning, when strolling on the terrace I saw tanks—three, four, five of them—pulling up at the entrance of the Royal Barracks.

Costa had gone out, I was alone in the house, and my only

hope was the radio. I turned it on, but it was still early and the gossipy European network had nothing to say about Athens. But news has a secret and swift way of traveling, and as I was gazing down I heard a workman who was painting one of the walls of a nearby apartment cry out: "Hey! The King has gone and dismissed the Colonels!"

Hanging over the terrace, I could not see anything really amiss. The tanks were there, and I took the Leica and photographed them, but people and cars were circulating freely, and no one seemed either afraid or excited. When Costa came back, earlier than usual, he did not know much. It was said that there had been a "royal coup," but in Athens information was still very vague. We had to rely again on the foreign radio stations, and they did not let us down. By two o'clock that afternoon we knew that King Constantine had left Athens, had issued a Royal Proclamation asking the military to surrender, and was now in Larissa, hailed by the people as a savior, with lighted candles, songs of joy, and genuine enthusiasm.

For a few hours that day we believed that the nightmare was over, that the King had won the Army back, and that the group of unlucky rebels would have to surrender any moment now. There would probably be an amnesty for most of the younger officers, as having been "influenced by their superiors." Karamanlis, freshly acquitted from any affiliation with the Junta by a recent declaration, would come back, and we would have to speed up preparations for publishing again.

This rosy vision faded in the early hours of the afternoon. The Greek Radio, which had kept a complete silence on the happenings, spoke out with sudden insolence. "The King has been misled by foolish adventurers. The Military Government is in full control of the country." We sat in front of our radio switching from one provincial station to the other, hoping to get a message from some "liberated" part of northern Greece, and meanwhile getting more and more confusing bulletins from the foreign stations. And there was not the slightest sign of unrest in the Athens streets. Most people seemed either not to know about the developments or not to care. The tanks were still posted outside the barracks, but the soldiers were strolling outside and talking with the royal guards, as if they were off duty.

It was a little later, when we heard the Greek Radio announce in a tone of confident sarcasm never used before that "Constantine is trying to save himself by running and hiding from village to village," that we realized the truth.

Just "Constantine"?

That was quite sufficient to make us understand that whatever the King had tried to do, he had failed. We did not know and could not imagine the magnitude of the failure, and the degree of lack of secrecy, thought, and preparedness that had made defeat almost inevitable. But we also saw it as a gesture of spirit and defiance, and whether it was a strategic mistake or not, it had been a mistake in the right direction.

But where was King Constantine now? The foreign stations had lost all contact with the group of the countercoup, nothing was heard from northern Greece, and names of arrested "royalist" generals were cropping up.

We stayed up all night, mostly sitting in the kitchen huddling over hot cups of coffee, always with the radio on, and it was in the early hours of the morning that we heard the final bad news.

"It has just been announced that the Greek Royal Family has arrived in Rome. King Constantine, with Queen Anne-Marie, Queen Mother Frederica, Princess Irene, and the royal children, accompanied by the Prime Minister, a retinue of courtiers, secretaries, and a nanny, flew from Greece in two regular Army planes provided by the Military Government."

We were aghast. Bad as the situation was before, this time it was infinitely worse. And the flight of the whole of the royal family was as incomprehensible as it was disastrous. What had happened? And how was it that they had been ready for that eventuality the very first day of the countercoup? Was it a fit of wild panic, a momentary aberration born from memories of mass executions of other royal families? But however undemocratic and stifling this police regime of ours was, it had not shown any signs of advancing toward bolshevik-type terrorism. Why leave Greece? Especially as the granting of planes by the Junta was the best of proofs that they wanted them to go. The Colonels had immediately realized how much they could exploit that royal exodus, and they were relieved to see the whole royal establishment out of Greece, together with Constantine Kollias, the Prime Minister they had tried so hard to get rid of.

It was not the King's failure, we felt, that the Greek people would not forget, but the immediate surrender that left the Colonels stronger and more confident than ever.

"Now, there is nothing more to wait for. What we were waiting for has happened, and it is over, and we are in a much worse situation for God knows how long, until new anti-Junta forces get together. Now, you must go!"

The very next day the prearranged signal was given, and the whole operation was accelerated. And the decision was taken. It would have to be tomorrow, Friday. They had found where to take me, a small flat with a telephone securely unknown and untapped.

It was not surprising that the choice had fallen on a rather disreputable *garçonnière*, a two-room basement where furtive comings and goings were the natural thing, though the lady visitors were not usually of my age and type. On my last day home, on the eve of the great adventure, I had very little to do. Nothing reminded me of past travel preparations: the only thing I had to pack was myself and a handbag. I tried to see how many jumpers and blouses I could put on one on top of another, in shoplifter's style, but that was about all, as I had to get out of the house dressed in everyday clothes so that if I was caught I could simply say that I was fed up with staying inside and had decided to go for a walk. No suitcases, no guessing what clothes would be needed, no good-byes, no telephone calls, no last-minute messages to practically everybody, family, secretary, friends; no looking over passports and checkbooks, address books, diaries of appointments to see if everything was in order; nothing to do but sit and talk and try to keep up a pretense of normality.

These hours were very difficult. We could not chase away the feeling that our life was being disrupted at the very roots and that a very pleasant companionship was being interrupted for a long time, if not forever. It was inevitable that we spoke about death. We were never afraid of talking about the eventuality that has to be included in everyone's future. We only had a major difference of opinion as to how it would be less unwelcome. Costa was of the "He was quite lucky, it was so sudden, he never knew he was dying" school, while I, on the contrary, disliked immensely the idea of being caught unawares, of missing my death, so to speak. I always felt that I wanted to know when the end was coming near, I wanted to put my getting out of life in order; and I remember drawing up wills when I was quite young and had little to bequeath except a lot of gratitude to people and to life in general. And I cannot say that we were helped by religion, or that we found consolation in belief in life after death. It always seemed to us wildly improbable that it would take any conceivable form, be any of the orderly paradises, hells, and purgatories that are so evidently inspired by life on earth.

Looking around the house, I realized that I had not finished any of the jobs I had started. I had not read the books I had put aside, I had not finished a rather vague short story, and I had not sorted and put in order all the photographs. Back they went into envelopes, drawers, boxes.

I put some of the photos aside, guessing that they could prove of future interest, and also chose a small collection of family pictures which I hoped could be sent to me at some future time. Traveling without the company of a familiar face made me feel more disembodied than traveling without my passport. Some reference books that could prove useful I put apart, together with the only copy I had left of a small book called *Mosaic*. This little book contained a number of articles of mine that had been published in the *Kathimerini* and translated into English.

If I had been an astronaut getting ready to settle on a faraway planet, I would not have felt more of a traveler toward the unknown. Not because of my destination's being distant, but because in all probability I would lose all contact with Greece and Costa. Even if he was not arrested after my escape, it would be extremely difficult to contact him by telephone, and quite impossible to speak freely if I did.

We had to think of everything during these last hours. Tonight I would be out of the house, and I could take nothing with me, and tomorrow I would try to get a suitcase and some clothes from friends, as I could not travel without some luggage. We had also to think of the maid. She would have to be provided with some explanation next morning when she would not find me in the house. "The Kyria felt sick during the night, and we managed to get her secretly out through the back door and take her to her own doctor's nursing home, so as not to go to a prison hospital. You are not to say anything unless you are asked"; that was the best we could devise, without hoping for a minute that she would believe it.

Our conversation that day was interspersed with "ifs" and with "don't forgets." "Don't forget to tell the children to write," and "If I get out of Greece safely, remember to send me the photographs. And some clothes; I have put the ones I want aside. I will show you. Don't forget the moment I am out to go on making exactly the same noises as if I were still in the house, and don't forget that you must go on pretending that I am inside the house as long as possible."

Then it was Costa's turn.

"Don't forget to be ready to leave the house exactly at the moment we hear the lift going down with the guard. Don't forget to stand on the left of the petrol pump, on Vassilissis Sofia, where the car will be at exactly twenty minutes to eleven. If something goes wrong, which is quite improbable, try to get there on foot. Don't forget the address."

After the maid left, we sat as usual in the living room, reading the foreign newspapers that were full of echoes of the dismal royal adventure. Later, as the time of my departure was approaching, we put both the dogs and the cat under lock and key, took a stroll on the terrace, confirmed that the night was dark and cloudy and also quite cold. The Athens weather can be full of surprises and the clemency of the climate is rather overrated, being usually confused with the uncontested perfection of the light. There must be few cities in the world bathed in the same brilliant, crystal clarity, and I always remember the remark of an ardent admirer, who used to say that when you leave Athens, you throw away the cellophane wrapper and you get the world as it is, dim and dull.

I tried very hard to swallow some dinner, and then I got ready. I put a handkerchief on my head and wore contact lenses, and that was all of my "disguise" that night.

I left the flat alone, at twenty past ten, and executing my part of the plan to the minute, found myself at exactly twenty minutes to eleven standing in Vassilissis Sofia Avenue, near the petrol pump, where there was no car to be seen.

I stood for four and a half interminable minutes on that pavement in the very heart of residential Athens. Scores of friends and acquaintances lived in the neighborhood, and I expected one of them to emerge any minute and to exclaim, full of joyful surprise, "Helen! You are out!"

But the car eventually arrived, and I was whisked to the "hideout" flat and abandoned there for the night. I don't know what I'd expected to find, but it was as far as possible from what I imagined a little lovenest to be. It was cramped, ugly, and bare, miserably furnished with cheap Scandinavian "modern" furniture, with lamps with weak bulbs under frilly discolored lampshades. The kitchenette was empty but for a solitary cockroach which scurried away as I came in, and in one of the wall cabinets there were some biscuits, half a bar of chocolate, and nothing else.

I sat wrapped up in my coat, more depressed than at any other time, feeling both miserable and ridiculous. I looked around for something to read and found on a bookshelf in the drawing room half a dozen of the dullest almanacs and novels —not one indecent publication amongst them. And I tried to visualize Costa feeling, probably, just as I felt, all alone in the Mourouzi flat, trying to convey the presence of two people to the guard sitting outside our door by producing all those "familiar noises" that we had written down. He had to put on the radio and the gramophone, call the dogs, open and close doors, run the water in my bath, walk around.

"I thought it would be quite easy to walk in those high-heeled slippers of yours," Costa said later, "and I put them on to make a realistic tap-tap sound like you did, but I very nearly came headlong twice as I tripped on the carpet."

Next morning two friends arrived, one by one, "certain of not being followed" in the best spy tradition, and they had brought coffee and sandwiches, and fruit and newspapers, and telephone numbers. I was to call three Ambassadors to begin with, the British, the American, and the French—the last with some special hope, as only a few months before the coup I had been decorated with full ceremony with the Ordre du Mérite, the only Greek journalist to have been so honored.

I had very little hope of achieving anything, but I knew that if I did not try I would always be accused of not having given them "a chance to help," so I got in touch with all three Ambassadors. As I could not give my name to the telephonist at the Embassy, I used in all cases names of common friends which I knew would bring their Excellencies to the other end of the wire.

"Who is calling please?"

"Lady Killearn."

"Hallo Nadine! Is that you?"

"Not exactly. . . ."

Nadine Killearn was a second cousin who had kept in close touch with the Greek side of her family. She was a delightful person, a mixture of her mother's Greek vivacity and the pleasant, friendly personality of her English father, Admiral Pilcher. Also, she had been lately in Athens and had come with Ambassador Michael Stewart to our Pendeli country house a month or so before I was arrested, so when I explained that I was "the cousin," he had no difficulty at all in placing me. He was sincerely appalled, and at a loss to see what he could do, and how he could help me to get out of the country. But he did ask me to ring him again that same afternoon.

That was more than I got from the American Ambassador, Philip Talbot. For him, I used the name of an old friend, Marina Sulzberger, an Athenian who had married the well-known American journalist, Cy Sulzberger, and who was one of the world's most charming personalities, perennially youthful in her thinking and appearance.

"Hallo Marina! I did not know you were here . . . !"

She was not, I explained, and this considerably damped his enthusiasm. It was me, and, as we knew each other quite well, he had no difficulty in recognizing my voice without naming any names. He was quite as appalled as Sir Michael and much more embarrassed. He did not even pretend to be able to think about helping me in any way. His one piece of advice was: "Why don't you try to contact a smaller embassy?" and to this day I don't know what he meant.

Via a terrified secretary I got through to René Bayens, the French Ambassador, who was on holiday out of Athens. There was nothing he could do either.

I refused to go on with more attempts, as this telephoning could prove quite dangerous. I did not go so far as to fear that my unwilling Ambassadors would give me away, but it was more than probable that their telephones were tapped, and that the dialogue could arouse suspicions. I had to get out of the country, and the quicker the better, so the false passport solution was the only one.

The friends left me before lunch to return dutifully to their homes, and they came back in the afternoon with "everything" ready. "Everything" was a suitcase with some clothes thrown in, collected from friendly feminine wardrobes, as I could not very well get through the customs with nothing but my handbag and a passport accompanied by the necessary police identity card. On both there was a woman's face which resembled mine in that it was the face of another female of the human race. We did not think it mattered much because passport photos are more credible when they do not look like their bearer, but she was a brunette, and something had to be done about that. Either a wig or a dye, and we opted for the second solution as being simpler. A box of Oreal, black, was bought from a central chemist.

By this time it was late afternoon on a Saturday, and there was nothing much to be done until Monday morning. I was left alone for the evening, but with plenty of comforts which had magically changed the character of the flat. I had provisions, masses of newspapers and magazines, and a small transistor radio. Only twenty-four hours had passed since I had left the Mourouzi flat, but already I felt as far away from it as if I had arrived in another country. I was also quite relieved with the decision to get away on my own, and that there was no one, either official foreigner or important Greek, involved. I only hoped that a ticket taking me from anywhere in Greece, by any form of transport, air, ship, or train, to somewhere out of Greece would be secured as quickly as possible, so that I could get away on Monday or Tuesday at the latest.

The next day, a Sunday, started and finished as a long briefing session. Friends and organizers were slinking in and out with ease as it was the porter's day off.

The subject of the debate was, where would I go, what would I do, what would I say? Everyone offered advice, repeated the message I had to give to the free world, drifted into past politics, and planned future solutions. It was a typical Athenian discussion, and only the hushed tones instead of the usual shouting gave it its conspiratorial atmosphere.

"Look," I said, "let us not exaggerate, and not hope for much. If I get out of Greece, I will do my best to contact as many people as possible, and just tell them the truth, which is bad enough to make any intelligent and honest man turn against the Colonels. But if the Greek people themselves don't help, if they just sit and wait for some magic force to shoo the military away, then the Junta will stay on, and the subject Junta will disappear from the foreign press. You know the old cliché: 'Dog bites man' is not news, but 'man bites dog' is. Well, it does not stop there, it goes on with 'man bites dog' is news the first time it happens, and maybe the second, but from then on he can go and swallow a St. Bernard for all the world will care. My telling that these men are ignorant and dishonest, ambitious and dangerous, is just an opinion, not news."

The chorus took over.

"If you go to America, try and make them see that one of the basic American mistakes is to believe that you control a military or dictatorial regime more easily than a democratic one. It is primitive Pentagon thinking based on one or two successful right-wing coups that have provided governments devoted to Washington. That they were the exceptions and not the rule passed unnoticed. The reason is simple. America uses democratic-looking methods to influence governments, tries to dictate through diplomatic and economic channels. Once a dictatorship is established, that kind of threat is just a joke. The displeasure of Washington is censored, and ignored, the sanctions create problems for the people but not for the well-entrenched military. With a democracy, with an opposition party sitting in the wings waiting to pounce, the displeasure of the big chief cannot be disregarded. The United

States practically controls many democratically run countries, but they are powerless against Castro. . . ."

"Greece without the Greeks is no use to the Western world, that is what you must tell them! We fought once, we are not going to fight again. Not if we find out definitely that our 'allies' believe that we should go and kill ourselves for *their* freedom and *their* democracy. . . ."

The group was composed of what one would call peaceful people, most of them well established and fairly successful, certainly not revolutionaries or Communists or even mildly left-wing. Yet in their bitterness and disappointment they were finding themselves completely isolated, surrounded by former allies that could as well have been enemies.

"Look, Helen, you just go and tell them simply: if this situation is allowed to go on, it will eventually deteriorate into civil war. Helped or not, sooner or later, we will throw the Junta out. . . ." I let them go on talking, as I was getting tired and confused and also increasingly anxious about the security of the hideout, what with the telephone calls and the comings and goings. My friends were just as worried, and on the spur of the moment I decided to leave and go, even if only for the night, to the Pendeli country house. If I was to be found out and rearrested, at least there I would be more respectable than hiding in that miserable rathole. And tomorrow, another shelter could be found.

Also we were satisfied that my absence from the Mourouzi flat had passed completely unnoticed. Every eight hours, at six in the morning, two in the afternoon and ten in the evening, the guards changed, sitting contentedly in front of the outside and inside doors, and taking good care that no unauthorized person "entered the premises." Their duty was to keep the visitors out, prevent anyone getting to me, rather than to keep me in. Probably they had not thought of the eventuality of my getting out. Most of the guards were very young men, and the few glimpses they might have had of me must have given them the reassuring picture of a tranquil, white-haired lady.

That evening in Pendeli we proceeded with the hair-dying operation, so that I would have something in common with the photo in the passport. We read the instructions most carefully, and emptied the contents of two different envelopes into a bowl, added water, and stirred. The result, a thick yellowish mixture, did not look as if it could dye anything black, and with a toothbrush in hand, we applied more and more of it. A little later, we were assured of success, as my hair was getting blacker by the minute. But this success was soon to be followed by disaster. Not only my hair, but my face was taking a new look. Evil black patches were appearing all over my forehead, my ears, my neck.

"Now we have gone and done it. You will never get through Health Control. You look like a leper."

We had passed half the night putting the hair dye on, and we spent the rest of it rubbing it off.

Meanwhile a new complication had arisen around the next day, which happened to be my birthday. Birthdays are not considered especially important in Greece, where the name day is the occasion for feasting and presents. But under the circumstances any pretext was good, and my mother weeks ago had asked for permissision to come and have lunch with me, with the birthday as an excuse. And permission, unfortunately, had been granted.

"Your mother was splendid . . . !" a friend told me later. "She came with flowers and a cake, and looked quite calm and happy, and even smiled at the guards."

The friend had also brought me the good news that a seat was booked on an air flight to Central Europe, for Mrs. X, and that she was due to leave the next afternoon. Meanwhile they had reserved a room for the night in a hotel near the airport, and I was to go there and lie low until it was time to come out into the open. Someone was going to be at the airport to see if I got away all right, but I was not to try to recognize him or to contact him in any way.

Later that day, I met Costa. This time it was the final parting. As we kissed good-bye, he pressed a little icon of Saint Nicholas into my hand: "Keep him with you. I had him with me all through the war. He saved me from the 'piano.' He is a good and lucky saint."

The "piano" was a macabre joke the Greek naval officers stationed in Alexandria shared during the war. One of the more hospitable Greek ladies, Kiki Salvago, had in her living room an imposing grand piano, on which she placed in heavy silver frames the photographs of Greek officers lost at sea. As the war progressed, the wish to "keep away from Kiki's piano" did not need any explanation.

From that moment on, I was on my own. I registered at the hotel, told the porter I was feeling tired and wished to have some dinner sent up to my room, left my passport and identity card so that he could fill in the necessary forms, and went up to a small but clean and comfortable room. I had nearly twenty-four hours to wait, but I had no intention of risking any budging from the room.

I did not know what was still in wait for me until the next morning, when a nice young man, a junior porter, brought my passport and papers back and said: "You know, your passport is not in order. If you want to travel. . . ."

If I wanted to travel!

As in most true stories of escape or any other unlawful if not dishonorable adventure, there had been a slip. The passport, which was supposed to be in perfect order, was not. An all-important detail had been overlooked, and "if I wanted to travel," as the young porter had so innocently put it, I had to see to it immediately. No, he was very sorry, he could not help me, the regulations demanded that I should go myself.

"You may be able to have it done and finished in the morning," he explained encouragingly. "Shall I call a taxi for you . . . ?"

There was not much that I could do but plunge into decision: "Please do."

As I started getting ready to go out, my predominant feeling was rage. What I wanted more than anything was to quarrel with my organizers, who had never stopped warning me to be careful, not to make mistakes, not to forget this, and not to overlook that, and who had let me in, at the very last moment, for getting right back into the city and trying to put a fake passport in order. But there was nothing else I could do. I either had to crawl back to Mourouzi Street or to give it a try.

A short drive took me to the given address, an imposing building in the center of the town, crowded with hundreds of compatriots, with regular police strolling everywhere, and probably quite a few "Security" around. I went to the information desk, stated my problem, and was told to go and queue at another department. There, after quite a wait, I got a whole mass of forms to fill in and sign. Name, parents, date of birth, profession, children. It was not the first time I had looked at the passport, and I was familiar with "my" biographical details, but there were gaps, and there was the problem of the signature which I had not envisaged. Hesitant at first, I grew more confident with every new form, and I finished by signing with ease and flourish.

But I got into trouble more than once.

"When did you last travel, Mrs. X?"

When had that woman traveled—or had she? I grabbed the passport back, turned the pages, and showed him some past visas with an idiotic smile. There, he could see for himself.

I finished with one department and queued in another. I was as terrified of being recognized as I was of seeing someone I knew. I was sure that the exchange of a glance would create some kind of recognition. By some miracle, during more than three hours I did not see one familiar face.

At one moment the question of foreign exchange arose. I was taking very little in the erroneous belief that the less money you had with you the less suspicious you looked. That was one more mistake. The clerk who noticed this, a nice old Greek, was not in the least suspicious, but just a bit worried. Would I have enough to live on? And how would I get back, seeing that I had no return ticket? I did a lot of explaining, talking of rich relatives who had invited me to be their guest, and this reassurance, together with the long line of people waiting in front of his desk, decided him. In a few minutes I had my passport signed, sealed, and stamped, together with a smile and a *"Bon voyage."*

"You see, it was not very difficult," the young porter said, probably wondering why women make such mountains out of molehills.

"No, it was not, you were quite right."

I thanked him and tipped him much less than I felt like, to keep in character. I was fervently grateful to him, as his little cameo role at the very last moment of the adventure had been a vital one.

The morning's ordeal had one good result. Three whole hours passed in the very middle of the crowded Greek offices had reassured me that this dowdy, heavily muffled woman, pale and drawn, with the raven black hair back-combed into a wild-looking nest, was a person who did not look like anybody anyone had ever seen before.

Later I learned that the friendly spy sent to witness my departure was amazed at the ease with which I sailed through all the formalities, answering quickly at the call of my new name, signing forms, looking the clerks right in the eyes. "It was true that I had to look twice myself to recognize her. She looked so awful!" he announced to the very proud and very relieved organizers.

I breathed freely for the first time in days only when I was airborne.

And then I had to fight conflicting emotions. Freedom, in its most intoxicating form, had suddenly been thrust upon me. After having almost none, I was now freer than ever before in my whole life, without definite destination, without appointments, without schedules, without people to see, jobs to do, family responsibilities, ties. Anxiety for the people back home brought a wave of remorse, but it was no use. At the moment I could not help a reaction of pure glee, a feeling of "having made it" which took me right back to the very young years when success in exams or in games, or the fulfilment of a wish, took on the burning quality of a personal victory. I could not help but think of the police still stolidly sitting outside our door, guarding me in Mourouzi Street, while I was flying over Europe.

During the flight, I pretended to think once again about where I was eventually going, considering Paris, Rome, New York, when I knew all the time in the back of my mind that it was to be London. I enjoyed the luxury of being able to balance the qualities of this capital against the offerings of the other, but it was in the way one looks again over an appetizing menu, after having decided what to order. I had not talked much about it before the escape, either with Costa or my helping friends, as they all felt that the important thing was to get out of Greece, and that the rest was irrelevant. But I think they all knew that it had to be London for a number of reasons, the principal one being that if one wanted to speak to the Western world, English was the language to do it in, and as a center of communication, London was unbeatable. The BBC was the world's best-heard radio voice, and what's more it spoke four times a day to Greece, in Greek. And the British press, even if it had lost part of its power, had kept most of its prestige.

For me there was an additional reason, and that was simply that I loved London. Paris and Rome were beautiful cities, but I was past monuments, buildings, and museums. It was the atmosphere of a city and the quality of its people that were the important thing, especially now, in what I knew would be a difficult and lonely time. I don't think that before the war I would ever have contemplated London in that fashion, but every trip out of Greece I had taken during those last years had convinced me that many prerogatives long considered European, like hospitality, gaiety, and friendliness, had left the Continent and crossed the Channel.

When the plane landed at an unfamiliar airport, I went directly to inquire about flying to London.

"You can make it if you hurry," the man at the desk said. "There is a plane leaving for London in twenty minutes."

It was dark and very cold when we arrived in London. In the bus riding from the airport to the city I marveled at the lights and the colors; and then, seeing a decorated tree, I realized for the first time that Christmas was only a few days away.

Only last year I would have been deep in preparations, sorting out the presents for the family, personnel, and friends, sending last-minute messages and Christmas cards, decorating the Christmas trees in the *Kathimerini* offices and at home, organizing family gatherings and festivities, worrying about the Christmas issues of the newspapers, and the social activities of both Christmas and New Year.

It was a measure of how much life had changed for me, that this year, for the first time in my life, I had forgotten Christmas.

INDEX

179